Social Anxiety Revealed

Miriam Drori

CROOKED
CAT

To Jane,

Hoping this book is useful for someone.

Miriam xx

Discover us online:
www.crookedcatbooks.com

Join us on facebook:
www.facebook.com/crookedcat

Tweet a photo of yourself holding
this book to **@crookedcatbooks**
and something nice will happen.

To Gill Downs,
who told me about SA
and did so much more
for me.

In Memory Of

D, who listened, understood and provided encouragement, and then sadly acquired problems of another kind.

Thanks

To Tracy, Gill, Dvorah, Jess, Hilary, Jane and David, for all their advice.

To Sue Barnard (my editor), and Laurence & Steph Patterson of Crooked Cat Books, for all their help and support.

And to all the anonymous contributors who agreed to have their words quoted in this book.

All these people have been invaluable in turning my writing attempt into a real book.

About the Author

Miriam Drori is the author of a romance, Neither Here Nor There, and co-author of The Women Friends: Selina, the first in a series of novellas based on a painting by Gustav Klimt. She is married with three adult children and enjoys folk dancing, hiking, touring and reading.

Miriam sees the publication of Social Anxiety Revealed as an important step in fulfilling an ambition that began in about 2003: to raise awareness of a condition that's very common yet little known.

Miriam has struggled with social anxiety for the past fifty years, although for thirty-five of those years, she didn't even know the name of it or that a name existed. Only recently has she come to the conclusion that she shouldn't have been struggling at all, but rather making friends with it.

In order to introduce this book and as a place for discussions with readers, Miriam has begun a blog that's devoted solely to the topic of social anxiety: **socialanxietyrevealed.wordpress.com/**. Everyone is welcome to visit and comment.

Social Anxiety Revealed

Chapter 1: Introduction
As important as the rest of the book.

Chapter 2: The Cast
The players in the book.

Chapter 3: What is SA?
A definition of social anxiety from different viewpoints.

Chapter 4: Why did it Happen to Us?
All the possible reasons.

Chapter 5: Symptoms of SA
What you see and what you don't.

Chapter 6: What We Find Hard
Reality for those struggling on.

Chapter 7: How We Feel
Feelings behind the reality.

Chapter 8: What We Want
What we want and struggle to get.

Chapter 9: What Helps
About therapy and other aids to coping.

Chapter 10: Advantages to Having SA
A short chapter.

Chapter 11: Solving the Problem
Advice for people who want to help.

Chapter 12: My Advice
Gleaned over the years, my advice for those with SA.

Appendix: Books and Links
A list of relevant books and websites.

Chapter 1
Introduction — Please Read

This introduction is as important to understanding this book as small talk is to getting to know someone. But who am I to talk of such things as small talk and social contact?

Attempting the Impossible

"Nothing's impossible," they say. But if I told you I wanted to fly across the Atlantic by holding on to a robin, you'd probably tell me that's impossible. So, is it possible for someone who doesn't have social anxiety (SA) to understand someone who does?

Presumably, for people who spend years studying it, understanding is possible. I would hope that someone whose job it is to help us would be fully aware of who and what they're dealing with.

But what about the average person in the street? How would she feel about the man in the office who hides behind his computer screen all day and won't join in office parties? How would he feel about the woman who blushes and stammers when all he said was "Can I help you?"

Even when we take the plunge and try to explain our SA to our spouses, parents, children, bosses and friends, results are varied. Sometimes we even feel it's helped the relationship as well as lifting a weight from our shoulders. But usually we decide that one has to have it to understand it.

I put this issue to Sofi, a psychologist from whom you'll hear more in Chapter 2.

"They can't understand," she said. "They see someone who is undoubtedly clever, yet whose self-confidence is," she stretched her arm down, her palm level with the floor, "grass-high, and it doesn't make sense to them."

In a previous interview, she explained the problem with this comparison: "Can you understand the difficulties of someone who has only one arm?"

I pondered the question long after I left her. In that sense, she's right – even more than right (even though I'm not suggesting that SA is as incurable as a missing arm). We see the problems of missing an arm. Although we take our two arms for granted, it doesn't take too much imagination to realise the difficulties such a handicap can cause, and to be aware that an arm is gone for ever. But SA is all in the head – a state of mind. How hard can it be, you might think, to change that state of mind?

But on another level, we have to get the message out that SA is very real. That it appears gradually without our noticing it, or before we're old enough to remember being different. And that once its spell has taken control, it requires a lot of hard work to get rid of it. As Sofi says, we have to publicise SA as much as possible, and especially to educate teachers and other people in responsible positions about SA and how it can and should be nipped in the bud.

My Mission

So why do I bother? Because I'd like to hope that it isn't impossible. I want to tell all I can about it in the only way I know how – in writing – and hope that I can fulfil one of my goals: to make SA understandable to the general public.

In so doing, I have another goal: to help people who are unaware they have it to come to the realisation that what they have has a name. That's the first step towards overcoming it. This book can help you to understand that you're not so weird and different. There are many more like you and me.

Everyone who makes this discovery says how good it feels to know there are plenty of others out there. So here's the message:

YOU ARE NOT ALONE!

And yes, I do see this as a mission. I'm passionate about increasing awareness of social anxiety for all the reasons mentioned here.

What Is Social Anxiety?

I've managed to get this far without even explaining what SA is. Here is a definition for now; a longer description appears in Chapter 3.

SA is an illogical fear of other people.

Sufferers of SA worry about what others think of them. The consequence of that is to clam up in order to block assumptions of thoughts that probably never existed.

In actual fact, I should refer to it as *social anxiety disorder*, because some people use the term *social anxiety* to describe a mild fear of public speaking. In my view, that's unfortunate, because it detracts from the attention that needs to be given to those who have the disorder. At the other extreme, viewing someone with social anxiety as a recluse (as in the book *The Mill River Recluse* that I review in Chapter 12) also provides a warped impression of social anxiety. But I'll stick with '*social anxiety*' because '*social anxiety disorder*' is a bit long and its acronym makes us sound pathetic.

What's in This Book?

This book is a description of SA, with personal examples of

what life is like for sufferers. It is intended for:

- People who have it but don't know what they have.
- People who know someone who may have it, but don't know what they have.
- Anyone who wants to know what it's like to have it.
- Anyone who knows what it's like to have it, and needs to be comforted by realising that they're not alone.

This isn't a typical self-help book with advice handed down by a qualified expert. It doesn't tell you how to get out of the SA rut, but it does include my advice for making peace with the beast. It tells you where else to turn for help. And it may inspire you to take the first painful steps.

It's also not academic. It's meant for the lay(wo)man. But I didn't call it *SA for Dummies*, because books with those titles may be OK for computers and fixing cars, but not for SA Sufferers. Personally, I don't find them OK for computers either. (When it comes to fixing cars, my dumminess has prevented me from even picking up such a book.)

In this book, quotes (mostly from others with social anxiety) are in boxes with a quotation mark (❝) in the top left corner, while humorous asides are in similar boxes with a triangle (▶).

Some Terms

Just to make sure we understand each other, especially as that's the purpose of our journey together, let's introduce a bit of jargon:

SA	Social Anxiety
SAer	Someone who has social anxiety

non-SAer	Everyone else
CBT	Cognitive Behavioural Therapy – the most widely accepted therapy for SA.

Other Things to Note

In order to discuss SA, I need to be able to distinguish between those who have SA and those who don't. In actual fact, there is no such clear-cut distinction. It is not possible to categorise people as one or the other.

The distinction is much more blurred and more of a continuum or spectrum.

In writing this book, I have had to make generalisations. In particular, I have assigned traits to SA sufferers that do not apply to everyone. We are all different, but it would get boring if I kept pointing that out.

The views expressed in this book are entirely my own, unless they're quoted from someone else. You're allowed to disagree with them, but please be careful how you do so. *You could cause me to retreat into my shell, lost in a sea of self-recrimination...*

Chapter 2
The Cast

SAers

Most SAers are terrified of being 'found out'. Even though for most of us it's pretty obvious that we have some sort of problem, being labelled with a disorder, particularly a mental one, is frightening. We are, by definition, afraid of what other people think of us, and don't want the added stigma attached.

My original idea was to include descriptions of and quotes from various SAers who would agree to appear anonymously. Several people expressed interest, but, as they introduced more personal information, some decided to drop out, and I came to the conclusion that the enterprise would be better off with quotes scattered throughout and not connected to one other. Most of these quotes were written in 2004, but are just as relevant today. Spelling and punctuation have been corrected in a few places where appropriate, but otherwise the quotes are reproduced exactly as originally written.

Some of the quotes were written specifically for this book. Others appeared in online SA forums and are presented here with the authors' permission. Posts on SA forums tend to be more coherent than many of those on other forums. That's because we take more care over them, and because SAers are intelligent people, despite all appearances to the contrary.

The Internet has indeed been a wonderful tool for SAers, as I can testify, and Chapter 9 has more about this. However, as I mention in Chapter 4, using the Internet as a replacement for face-to-face encounters is undesirable.

Non-SAers

Almost the only non-SAer who appears in this book is Sofi:

Sofi Marom, PhD, a senior psychologist and expert in cognitive behavioural therapy (CBT). She ran the group therapy that I attended, and specialises in social anxiety. In response to my questions, she told me that she has been helping people with SA for over twenty years, having chosen that field and method of therapy for several reasons.

"People with social anxiety are nice," she said. "And they usually don't know that it is possible to get help for their problems. They usually respond well to therapy, and I enjoy being able to help them."

Over the years, Sofi has run courses for well over a thousand people. According to tests that she gave the participants before and after the course, nearly 50% improved by 50%, and 42% improved by 60%. Participants are monitored over an eight-year period following the course, and this shows further improvement. Surprisingly, the results are not connected to the age of the participants.

"I get a lot of feedback from people who are extremely thankful," said Sofi. "They tell me about all the things they have started doing. The last group included three lawyers, who have since started to work again. Some phone me a long time after the course and report not just on the things they have been able to do but also on a complete change of lifestyle."

"CBT has developed since your day," Sofi told me. "It now includes behavioural experiments. There are also more therapy opportunities for children."

About Me

In a course on assertiveness and emotional intelligence, I heard of a French expression that seemed to relate to me: "*ne pas se sentir dans sa peau*" (not feeling good in one's skin). I tried to find a similar expression in English, and the best one seemed to be "living a lie", which is a bit off-putting when you've always thought that lies are bad. But this lie is one that I haven't told on purpose. What I mean is that the person you see on the outside isn't the one on the inside. I suppose that's true of any SAer. But it's truer for those who remember being different, however long ago that might have been.

I remember being an outgoing child. I was never afraid to talk to anyone. SA appeared around the age of fourteen. It comes up on you gradually, like a snake wrapping itself around you while you sleep. By the time you notice it, it's too late to shake it off. I've lived with SA ever since, although I only discovered the term at the age of almost fifty.
It could have been worse, as you'll find out later.

Why Me?

Now I'm sixty-three, and for the past eight years I've been open about who I am, online at least. It took a while, but I finally came to the conclusion that I wouldn't lose much by coming out, so to speak, and announcing to the world:

"I'm Miriam and I have social anxiety. Inside that quiet, shy and boring exterior that you see is a lively and interesting person trying to get out."

Should that be more than "trying"? Succeeding? Some would agree; others wouldn't.

Another quality qualifies me for writing this book: I'm not inherently shy. In the words of computer jargon, usually SA comes packaged with shyness. I got the stand-alone version. People who know me (or think they do) are often amazed at things I do. I like to dance at the centre of a crowded hall where everyone can see me. I enjoy giving presentations where all eyes are on me. (But I don't always like answering the questions afterwards – that requires spontaneity.)

I've already made a name for myself as an author of fiction. So I think I'm ready for the acclaim I hope to achieve by writing this book. And the more laurels my book wins, the more people – SAers, non-SAers, and those who don't know what all this means – will hear and possibly understand.

Chapter 3
What is SA?

> **Pet for Sale**
>
> Name: Social Anxiety
>
> Formerly: Social Phobia
>
> Nickname: SA
>
> Date of Birth: 1980
>
> Food: No need to buy food. It eats your self-confidence.
>
> Equipment – cage: No need for cage. In fact it will build a cage for you using no raw materials. No one will be able to see the cage, but everyone will feel it.
>
> Equipment – leash: No leash required; it will never leave your side.
>
> Uses: It will prevent you from being too relaxed, free and happy by manipulating your thoughts.
>
> Price: Nothing. In fact the owner is prepared to pay you to take it away

"You don't have to feel sorry for him," someone said to me once before she realised whose side I was on. "It's his own choice whether to talk or not." I looked at her in disbelief and didn't say a word. I have SA, you understand.

So to that woman and to everyone else, this is something I can't emphasise enough:

NO ONE CHOOSES TO HAVE SA.

If we'd known what was coming to us, we'd have done everything in our power to avoid it. But we didn't. We were only young. We couldn't know how one little action could lead to more that could eventually have such an effect on us.

Description

> ▶
>
> **Mind-reading lessons**
>
> Do you want to know what other people are thinking about?
>
> Lessons in mind-reading from Miriam Drori, S.A., a self-taught mind-reading expert.

SA is an illogical fear of other people. It can be all others, most others or only a few others. It is always accompanied by automatic, often irrational thoughts about what the other person is thinking.

SAers tend to worry about an upcoming event, imagining what could go wrong at it. Afterwards we analyse it in detail, again imagining what the other people are thinking of us.

> ▶
>
> Ever stop to think, and forget to start again?

If you are now thinking, "What's all the fuss about? We're all like that," read on. Actually, read on, whatever you're thinking.

Is SA Shyness? Is Shyness SA?

That's a hard one. Personally, whenever anyone has called me shy, I have thought that that attribute shouldn't be applied to

13

me. But how could I say so when I was so quiet and obviously afraid of talking? Most SAers are also shy and trying to distinguish between the two confuses everyone.

This is what SAers have written:

> 66
>
> The answer to the question what's the difference between social anxiety and shyness has been going on for ages. Is there a real answer?
>
> I say that I have SA but am not shy because when I do feel relaxed I can be reasonably outgoing. At times the SA isn't really an issue. I would never describe my personality as introverted but the SA sometimes hides it, so it does probably seem like I am shy.
>
> Then again I don't know enough about shyness really to compare the two, what is shyness? I always thought shyness was more a part of your personality whereas SA isn't? so I don't know what I am going on about lol.

> 66
>
> Ok, to me being shy is something that is ascribed to someone who has initial problems communicating "she's shy until you get to know her..." it's a temporary state before "warming" to others.
>
> People have said to me "I just thought you were shy" but they soon realise I'm not shy because no matter how much they harp on I still don't melt.
>
> Also I see being shy as a personality trait. There are a few people I'm not "shy" around and some situations that don't make me "shy".
>
> Social anxiety for me is something that can happen in a moment. I can go from having a laugh with a well trusted friend to the middle of a situation (say a stranger asking me for the time) and suddenly feel my SA take hold.

Another disorder that overlaps with SA is called APD (avoidant personality disorder). Avoidance in SA returns in Chapter 5.

Analogies

It might help to compare SA to something more tangible.

Take your pick:

- A wall. You can't see it but you have to stay behind it. In the song *Something So Right* by Paul Simon, the Great Wall of China is compared to the imaginary wall surrounding the singer, similarly built to keep out foreigners, even though it's invisible. That song has been speaking to me ever since I first heard it.

▶

Some thoughts about walls

Walls have ears, they say… but they don't have mouths.

When we fail to reply, people feel as if they're *talking to a brick wall.*

Why is it the idiot in Shakespeare's *Midsummer Night's Dream* who plays the part of the wall? Perhaps it's because the wall surrounding me makes me seem like an idiot.

- A cage that keeps you imprisoned although you can see the outside world.
  In *The Zürau Aphorisms*, Franz Kafka writes about a cage that searches for a bird. That's exactly how SA feels. Like Kafka's active cage, it lands so that it surrounds you, and takes away your freedom.
- A screen – like the wall and the cage.
- A force pushing you back whenever you want to get

15

close to anyone.

- A glass box: you can hear and see the world, but can't interact with it.

- An unwanted visitor, who just turns up. You realise it's thinking of staying, but you don't know how to get rid of it. It's hard work. Sometimes you think it's gone, but then it comes back.

- A computer virus: you don't realise it's there until you find you can't do things you used to do. Then you have to work hard to get rid of it.

- Drowning:

> I can only seem to ever make sense of how I feel by coming up with vague analogies to describe what's going on. So, I thought of this...
>
> I feel like I'm drowning, and when I'm under the water I can't make any noise that anyone can hear, and no-one above the water can see me underneath, and the only people that can see me are drowning too so they can't help me. So sometimes I struggle to the surface, and then people can hear and see me, and I can try and ask for help but all I can do is give a second-hand explanation of what it's like to be drowning, and because I'm above the water I don't look like I really need help. The only time I can express how I'm feeling is the time when I need help the least. But then I go under again, and the whole thing repeats itself.

Does that make sense to anyone? That, at the times you really need help, you have no way of asking for it or even expressing how bad you feel. And you have to wait till you're at your 'best' (relatively speaking) before you can do anything about it, but at which time you don't actually need it as much...

I s'pose it's like having SA and feeling too scared to go out the house, and the only time you can see a doctor to tell them things are so bad is when the anxiety is at its least severe and you actually are out the house so you'll just get ignored anyway.

How do you tell someone that you don't know how to tell them what you need to tell them? How do you express the fact that you can't express yourself without contradicting yourself and looking stupid?

"

[Referring to the previous quote]

That totally makes sense to me. To be underwater most of the time makes it hard to explain to someone what it's like when you finally surface. I think maybe it's because when you do surface, you almost want to deny what it was like to be drowning, you want to enjoy your time at the surface and maybe even believe that it is the start of something good. Your view of drowning becomes blurred and your explanation of what it is like is unconvincing, which means, unfortunately, that people may see you as not being in need of help. Then it all slips away, and you fall under and start drowning again, with absolutely no way of telling someone what it's like, because you are not able to connect – you just wish you could have done when you had managed to surface.

> I can absolutely relate to that. I felt like I was drowning for years, since I was about 15, and now, at 21, I seem to be treading water more and more, with my head above the surface. Because of this, I've been able to tell people what it's been like, for the first time in my life. I slip under often, but not all the time. I so wanted to tell people about my problems for years, but I was in no position to do it – I didn't even know what was wrong with me, just that I felt exactly the same way that you've just described.
>
> Anyway, it seems like you do have a clear idea of what your predicament is (albeit, only when you're in a depressive state and unable to speak to anyone about it), and obviously you want help. Maybe you should write down some of your thoughts and show them to someone when you do find that you're able to connect?
>
> ...and yes, that's an excellent way of describing it.

- A fire trap:

> ❝
> SA is like being trapped in a room where the escape door is blocked by a fire. Many of us remain trapped because we just try to stay in the corner furthest from the fire. We have to go through the fire accepting that we will get a little burnt but realising we can take it and it's the only way to escape.

Here's another analogy. What's the thing you've done that has scared you the most? Let's say it's standing on the edge of a cliff. Imagine standing there by yourself, looking all the way down to the sea, knowing that one wrong step will be the end. Imagine how you feel, your heart racing, your hands shaking.

Now imagine having to walk out and stand on that cliff for

five minutes, fifty times a day, every day of your life.

Antonyms

I once had to stand for a long time at a bus stop, waiting for a bus that didn't turn up. There were many other people waiting, too. They were all fairly quiet, except for one girl who had Down's Syndrome. She was talking to herself in an extremely loud voice, so that all the others couldn't help listening.

"Are you coming home today?"

"Yes."

"What time will you arrive?"

"I don't know. About 5 o'clock."

And so on. In the middle she would suddenly ask me the time and talk about the bus that still hadn't arrived. Then she would return to her diomonologue.

What are you thinking about that story? You're probably thinking, "Poor girl."

That's what I thought at the time. But later on, I thought again. That girl was the exact opposite of an SAer. She could do things that other people thought totally weird without caring what they thought; she wasn't suffering.

Contradictions

I've often found it hard to understand myself. I can dance in the centre of a crowded room without caring whether anyone is watching me, or perhaps even hoping that they are. I can give a presentation that I prepared in advance, and even enjoy the sound of my voice. Yet I can't talk to anyone without sounding scared. In 2004, when I wrote the first draft of this book, I said: *I don't know how to share my feelings with anyone, possibly even myself.* I think I'm better at that now, although extracting the feelings is still a struggle.

Unlike me, most SAers don't like to like to be the centre of attention. But SA causes contradictions in all of us.

> "
> I am alone yet I am not a loner.
> I want to be loved yet I push people away.
> Internally I'm strong yet outwardly I'm weak.
> I have an ego yet I feel inferior to others.
> I can be self-absorbed yet always prefer to talk to someone about themselves rather than myself.
> I find myself thinking of a way to gain pity yet hate it if someone shows pity towards me.
> I don't like being the centre of attention yet I crave anyone's attention.
> I'm not tactile yet long for human touch.

> "
> I read somewhere that people with SA are quiet people who are not naturally quiet. The reason we fight against our 'shyness' is because we have things we want to say, but can't get the words out, whereas naturally quiet people have no real desire to express their thoughts to people. So we really feel we DO have decent things to contribute, and are outraged at our inability to do it.

> I want company, but company that understands me and company that I feel relaxed around. When you seek this and fail to find it, you can feel even more alienated and hence don't want company. You oscillate between the two extremes without ever finding a balance.

> Wanting to please others but wanting to stand up for myself. Similarly, wanting to be accepted but not wanting to have to compromise on who I am to achieve that.

> Say I talk to someone and make them laugh and enjoy myself ... and I feel great, I was fine .... Afterwards I find it hard to talk to the same person again, because I don't want to spoil the good impression I made. Then I feel bad because I've been avoiding them ...

* Feeling I'm intelligent and understand a subject well, but hiding that as much as possible, and even pretending I don't know anything about it, so that people won't correct me and discover that I'm less clever than them.
* Being able to talk about very personal things with people I don't know, like on the Internet, or people I'm sure I won't meet again, but being unable to talk about those things with people close to me, like close friends, family and even the psychologist, because I'm afraid it'll affect the way they relate to me.
* Feeling relieved every time I manage to avoid meeting people I'm afraid of (people I don't know at work, in shops, on the telephone ...) and someone else does the job for me. The conflict is that this relief is even more than the achievement I feel if I manage to accomplish the task.

SA Survey

Someone conducted a survey amongst SAers. Like the polls that appear later, it has no meaning statistically but is interesting nonetheless. We'll be discussing causes of SA, depression and other issues mentioned here.

41 people filled in the questionnaire.
Of those people, 37 were white, 1 Chinese, and 3 other.
20 people were female, 21 male.
15 people have as yet received no professional help with their SA.

1. At what age did you develop SA?

6 people said they've always had it. Out of the others, the average age was 12½, but ranged from 4 to 19.

2. How has it changed over time (eg got worse)?

14 people said their SA had got worse, and 6 felt it had got better. The remainder said it had gone up and down.

3. What do you blame for your SA (eg genetics, experiences, etc)?
17 people felt their experiences were fully to blame, and 3 people blamed genetics. The remainder thought both were to blame.

4. Have you always been shy?
31 people said they suffer from shyness and have for most of their lives, if not all of it.

5. What's your main problem with SA (eg talking to strangers, blushing, etc)?
There were many mixed answers here. The most common were talking to strangers, talking to people in authority, avoiding behaviour, and blushing.

6. Do you, or have you, suffered from depression?
A massive 39 people answered "yes" to this question.

7. Have you formed many friendships/relationships whilst having SA?
Few relationships were mentioned in this section, and many people felt the only friendships they'd made were online. 9 people said they've never had a friend. Most other people have had few friendships.

8. Would you describe yourself as a paranoid person?
24 people said "yes". Most other people said they did to an extent, apart from 9 people who said "no".

9. Have you received help for your SA? If so, what?
15 people have received no help with their SA. 17 people take, or have taken, meds. A few people had seen counsellors or gone through CBT therapy. 3 people said they are still waiting for CBT or therapy. A couple of people had tried hypnotherapy.

What Non-SAers Think of the Description

- That's just shyness. Lots of people are shy.
- I don't have many friends either.
- Get out more, snap out of it.
- I know someone else with anxiety. He said there's this book that really helps. Check it out...

OK. For argument's sake, I'll agree that SA can be shyness. But shyness isn't always, or even usually, SA. When does shyness become SA? When it takes over your life. When it stops you from doing the things you really want to do.

You may not want many friends. If you do, there are many other problems that may hinder you in your search for friends. That doesn't make SA invalid.

Snap out of it? Would that it were so easy. If only I could just decide that other people's thoughts don't matter; that I can express myself as well as anyone else; that I am an interesting person and other people want to hear me, and then snap out of it. It doesn't work like that. Taming SA is much harder than that.

And that recommended book on anxiety? Social anxiety is not general anxiety...

Differences between Social Anxiety and General Anxiety (GA)

- Thoughts that lead to anxiety. Someone with GA worries about situations and relationships. Someone with SA worries about what others will think of them.
- GA usually appears intermittently and sufferers never know what might set it off. SA is more regular. Certain people will always cause it. Certain situations will always cause it. You might think that makes it easier to handle. But it can also be a reason for avoidance. If you know a situation will cause anxiety, you don't want to go through with it.
- These differences can lead to different behaviours.
- Usually, if GA can be treated enough to vanish or retreat into the background, the problem is solved. With SA, anxiety can be treated, but learned behaviours don't go away with the anxiety.

What Non-SAers Think of Us

We have been accused of being stupid, rude, lazy, gay, laid-back, cowardly, nice, egotistic, stuck-up and weird.

Stupid

It makes sense. We don't know what to say or how to behave, so we appear stupid. But if you could see all those complicated thoughts going through our heads, you'd know there must be some intelligence in there.

Rude

> **"**
>
> Looking through the messages on this site, there are several things that crop up time and again, and one of them is the question of rudeness, and how often "normal" (ie non-SA) people consider us to be rude because we don't speak, we hide in our rooms, we don't socialise, we don't make eye contact etc.
>
> And yet we never intend to be rude, in fact we're trying not to be, and are somehow afraid we'd be seen as rude if we "butted in" and actually put ourselves forward!

Lazy

> **"**
>
> I have been told to pull myself together on more than one occasion by my mother-in-law. (She thought I was just lazy until I got the courage up to tell her otherwise.) But I don't think she really understands what it's like to have SA; I don't think anybody does unless they suffer from it.

> I wish I knew which I was; my family think I'm a lazy bastard.
>
> But the thing is, I'm at ease around them most of the time and in a separate room for a lot of that time, so they don't see the side of me that blushes in public, the side of me that wants to hide when out on my own or the way I constantly seem to be in a rush to get away from anywhere crowded, or any of my other odd behaviour.
>
> It's irritating to hear I'm a lazy bugger all the time...
>
> Sometimes I believe it and that just depresses me even more.

> I think I'm quite lazy at the moment, but it's just due to a lack of motivation caused by a lack of belief in my own ability – caused by the SA. So I just don't try now. I used to be very motivated and hard-working, so I don't think I'm naturally lazy.

Gay

SA men, in particular, have a hard time finding girlfriends. Even in this day and age, men are expected to make the first move, and a lack of self-esteem makes that difficult. If people you know think you're gay, just because you don't have a girlfriend, the job of finding one doesn't get easier.

> Once my feelings of awkwardness and shyness made me too nervous when I was with a girl and it led to (ahem) temporary erectile dysfunction. She asked (probably in kindness) if I wasn't sure I was gay. People who vaguely know me as a family friend or far-off relative have been known to ask this too.

> **"**
>
> I'm sick of people thinking I'm gay because I haven't got a girlfriend. It's really starting to *** me off. So what if I haven't got a girlfriend? That doesn't mean I'm gay. I still fancy women. I just find it hard talking to them, but you can't explain that to the *** around here. If you haven't got a girlfriend you must be gay. But do they see me going with men? No they *** don't. I would love to have a girlfriend but I'm not going to try and get one to prove I'm not gay, I'll just wait till I meet the right person for me.

Laid-back

> **"**
>
> At school and to a lesser extent at work, I used to be called that, in fact it has been said to me "If you get any more laid-back, you'll be comatose!" I don't think people said it because I lacked confidence (even though I did). I think it was because the outward impression I gave was one of being quite nonchalant about things. I would go with the flow and just shrug my shoulders. What they didn't realise was that this was a defence mechanism – I would pretend not to care about things and then I couldn't get hurt. At home where the real me came out I was considered to be a "nervous wreck!" – just shows you, don't judge a book by its cover!

> I've been described as being "laid-back" on several occasions, particularly when I was at school. I don't think it had anything to do with my lack of confidence, although it was clear for anyone to see that I hadn't got an ounce of confidence. It was probably because I was very easy-going at school and never seemed fazed by anything anybody said, particularly when people were taking the p* out of my shyness (despite not showing any external emotion, the p*-taking tore me to bits really). In reality, I'm anything but laid-back, despite outward appearances – how can I be laid-back when the simplest tasks have my stomach in knots?

Timid, Cowardly

I understand that we seem timid and cowardly, but in fact we're just the opposite. Just by being there and facing you, we are being very brave. It may seem like nothing to you, but we have come from a different place.

Nice (as in "people pleaser")

> 'Nice' is a sucky word. I always think people are criticising me when I'm described as nice. Conjures up boring, bland for me.

> Compliments become stale if you're giving them all the time... I suppose it can seem that you're under-representing your 'darker' side if you never show it, if you never take the risk of being found even remotely egregious, or just generally never show a natural, human 'edge.'

> Girls only ever want to be friends [not girlfriends] with the nice guy. Despite what they say. The whole "nice" or "nasty" issue is far from clear: they are relativistic terms having little concrete grounding. For example, psychologically there are good reasons not to trust somebody that is always "nice".

Many SAers will do anything to be liked, even at the expense of their own needs. Putting other people first can cause them to feel frustrated, and even angry and resentful of those who exploit their "niceness". But they continue because they want to be liked. Being a people pleaser, however, doesn't bring the friendships they crave.

Other people see nice people as ... well ... nice. They're good to you and helpful. They don't complain when you ask them to do your job. They sympathise when you're upset, providing a shoulder to lean on. But would you choose a nice person as a close friend? No, you'd choose someone with a personality, someone you can have fun with, someone you can identify with.

Our attempts to be liked just lead to rejection.

Egotistic

This label has some truth. These people were discussing the suggestion that shyness is just egotism out of its depth.

> I never really thought about it before, but in my case it certainly makes a bit of sense. I must be quite egotistical really because I regard myself as being so significant that I automatically presume everyone else is analysing me to the same extent that I analyse myself, when in reality they don't give a damn. Maybe my ego and self-obsession is the actual cause of my SA.

SA people are more likely to negatively perceive their actions, intents and thoughts. To believe their thoughts, actions and intents are egotistic would fit into the nature of SA. It depends how egotism is defined. I mean, having self-assurance of yourself and your abilities, is this egotistical? Taking pride in your work or appearance, is this egotistical? Maybe shy people like me are uncomfortable with these things, but that could be more of an attribute of self-esteem than because of what could be perceived as egotistic reasons. When talking to a counsellor, I said something like that I believed talking about yourself was egotistic, a belief she managed to convince me is untrue.

However, on the other side of the coin, I know I have internally criticised people before, and that has set off anxiety. To criticise someone, I think, is to believe you are better than them, so I think to this extent egotism is a factor in my anxiety, although I am more doubtful about attributing it to shyness, since some people are born shy by nature. Some children are shy, as I was, and this has continued into adulthood.

My third point on the subject, which I came up with in some weird mood, is that egotism is a defence. Perhaps, because I lack certain social skills, my actions could be perceived as egotistic. When you hold onto a belief or viewpoint, say for example for dealing with something, another person might disagree and think it should be done another way. You can't think of a way of explaining your belief/viewpoint, but continue to hold that belief or do things that way. To the other person, this could be perceived as egotistic.

Stuck-up

> At least two temps from our office declared me arrogant because I didn't chat to them. The real reason is half not being confident enough to chat to them and half not thinking they want to know me at all.

> I worry they may think that [I'm stuck-up]. [Really it's] shyness – fear of failure/success/rejection/attention.

> Sometimes people think I'm stuck-up. Really I'm afraid – I'm not even sure why, as it's illogical. It's more a feeling of claustrophobia when there are a lot of people. It's as if I feel everyone together and I'm squashed inside.

> Often people around me who are a bit spiteful and see that I'm quiet say, "She probably thinks we're idiots because we joke around," although really I want to join in with them but can't let go.

Weird

Imagine you have a neighbour who lives on his own. (I have made him male because it seems that more male than female SAers live alone.) You don't know anything about him, despite having discussed him with the other neighbours, because no one seems to know him at all. You have caught glimpses of him leaving or returning to his house, but you haven't been able to catch his attention because he always goes in and out as quickly as possible, looking straight ahead.

So one day, being a friendly person, you decide to accost him. 'Accost' is the wrong word really. You don't see it like that at all, but he does. You just stand in his path, so that he can't pretend he hasn't seen you, and say:

"Hi. I'm John, your neighbour. I thought it was about time we met."

He blushes and looks down at his feet.

You try again. "I'm John, your neighbour. What's your name?"

He blurts out his name and hurries into his house, dropping his key in the process.

By this time you have formed a distinct opinion of your neighbour. He's weird.

You'll probably report back to the other neighbours and everyone will know that he's weird. I don't blame you. Most people don't behave in that way, and so it's natural that you should regard him as weird.

But we don't regard ourselves as weird. We have the advantage of knowing why we behave as we do. We know we don't behave like other people, but our behaviour is a logical result of our thoughts, which are a logical result of our life experiences. (The thoughts themselves are often illogical in the context in which they occur, but make sense against the SAer's own background.)

Why is SA Not Well-Known?

As a known mental disorder, SA is relatively new, as it was recognised only in the 1980s. Also, by definition, SAers talk less than other people and find it particularly hard to discuss their problems. Many live in fear of being "found out" and feel this is the worst thing that could happen to them.

Perhaps they're right. Those who manage to hide their feelings and appear "normal" on the outside may well lose credibility, friends, jobs and more by admitting to suffering from a mental disorder. On the other hand, hiding SA is like hiding details of the place where you live – like hiding a part of you. And keeping secrets involves telling untruths, which in turn can often lead to complications.

Nevertheless, some people are surprisingly willing to listen without judging. SAers have to pick their audience carefully and try to explain in a way that others can understand. Bottling up thoughts and emotions fosters SA. Pulling out the cork can be another step towards loosening its knots.

This is a blog post I wrote in May 2009:

"

I'm not gay, but I'm coming out. The process has taken about seven years so far and I still don't feel comfortable saying, "I have Social Anxiety."

"What's that?" is the typical response. No one asks that about being gay. Once the statement is made, it's understood. Gayness … gaiety… homosexuality has become an accepted state. Similarly, depression is mostly understood. No one has to ask what depression is.

So what is it with SA? Why don't people know about it? The definition of SA provides the answer. SA is a fear of people and particularly of what those people think of the sufferer. People with SA tend to avoid talking to others and often avoid social contact altogether. So other people don't know they exist, or they don't know what they're thinking, why they're so quiet.

That's why SA doesn't get the recognition it needs – we need – to fight it, destroy it, prevent it from starting even.

Why has it been so hard to come out? Because I'm afraid of the response. Afraid of the thoughts, even if they're not spoken. Afraid of being thought strange, weird. It goes against my unwritten, unplanned life policy: to pretend to be the same as everyone else. It's an impossible quest. You can't miss out on so many basics of growing up and still behave in the accepted way in every situation. And yet, I still try to do it. And I imagine that by keeping quiet I'm not "found out," although I know that this is untrue.

Chapter 4

Why did it Happen to Us

These are two polls I posted. As you can see, my wish to include the results in the book became a reality.

Two polls for the price of one. I don't know whether either will work out. If they do, I might put the stats in my book.

What is the main experience that caused your SA? (44 votes)	
Sexual abuse	3 = 6.82%
Physical abuse by adults	1 = 2.27%
Psychological abuse by adults	2 = 4.55%
Living in a dysfunctional family	2 = 4.55%
Learned behaviour	5 = 11.36%
Bullying by other children	12 = 27.27%
Bullying by teachers	1 = 2.27%
Being made to feel different	1 = 2.27%
Trauma	1 = 2.27%
Another bad social experience	1 = 2.27%
Drugs	0 = 0.00%

Alcohol	0 = 0.00%
A mixture (no single answer stands out)	9 = 20.45%
Nothing identifiable	6 = 13.64%

[Note: Sometimes, in an attempt to find a simple explanation of why they're suffering, people might choose reasons that aren't true, because the real reasons are harder to accept or just aren't apparent at all.]

Like the first, but this time you get to rate all the options from 0-10: 0=not at all, 10=a lot. (This is more fun than the statistics course I hated at uni.)

How much did these factors contribute to the onset of your SA? (41 votes)	
Sexual abuse	1.88 (Avg)
Physical abuse by adults	2.41 (Avg)
Psychological abuse by adults	4.20 (Avg)
Living in a dysfunctional family	4.61 (Avg)
Learned behaviour	5.66 (Avg)
Bullying by other children	6.80 (Avg)
Bullying by teachers	2.85 (Avg)
Being made to feel different	6.83 (Avg)
Trauma	3.88 (Avg)
Another bad social experience	4.68 (Avg)

Drugs	2.49 (Avg)
Alcohol	1.83 (Avg)

Childhood: A time to laugh and jump and play. A time to have fun... Or is it?

Some SAers don't know why they caught SA. Either it was always there, or it started growing apparently from nothing.

But most of us have a pretty good idea. We can point to other family members with similar problems. We can highlight experiences, especially childhood experiences from inside and outside the home, that had profound and negative effects on us. Some of us can blame things we have done to ourselves. Often we can do all of those.

No one is saying that anyone who had similar experiences would necessarily catch SA. We are all different and react to the same circumstances in different ways.

I hope you like the term: to *catch* SA. I like it because just as no one in their right mind would want to catch a physical illness, no one sets out to catch SA.

Genetics

> "
>
> I am not open with anyone in my family. I have 3 brothers and sisters and none of them has ever had a partner. My parents also have hardly any friends and my mother is quite suspicious of anyone who tries to get near them. No one in the family is strong at interpersonal communication, and I'd say that the family, as a body, tries quite hard to be a substitute for relationships with people outside it.

> No one else in my family had SA, and that's why they didn't know how to help me, I think. SA is something you're born with and it's made worse by experiences at home. As time passes, if it's not dealt with, it gets worse and worse, and the older we get the harder it is to get out of it. I know that even if I work hard on myself, I'll never get rid of SA. That's something you have to learn to live with, for good and for bad.

Like father, like son, like the short-rolling apple; we are the products of the people who created us and there's nothing we can do about it. So if we have SA, we can probably point to other family members who have, had, or probably had SA.

Often it's hard to tell whether the causes are genetic or copied. Most of us grow up living with the people who created us. Behaviours could be inborn or learned, sometimes even before we remember learning them. It doesn't really matter which. I'm not about to suggest that children of SAers should be taken away from their parents. What of children of non-SAers who are brought up by SAers? There are two quotes about this later in this chapter.

Unlike the author of the second quote above, I don't think anyone is born with SA. I think all SAers are born with a disposition towards SA, but probably many who have the disposition never catch it, because they don't experience events that awaken it. Once SA is caught, does it remain forever? In other words, do I agree with the statement: "I'll never get rid of SA" in the second quote above? I'll return to that question later.

Experiences

One characteristic that is common amongst SAers is sensitivity. We take things to heart, whether they're good or bad. The things that caused SA were bad. SA can be sparked off by something as simple as moving house. But usually the cause is more complicated.

Childhood Abuse

I think everyone can understand this, even those (including me) to whom it hasn't happened. Any child who has constantly been told they're no good from before they can remember will grow up thinking that they're no good. Any child who has grown up without love will find it hard to give or receive love. Any child who has experienced abnormal behaviour in the home environment will exhibit that same behaviour or (conversely) be afraid of exhibiting it.

> **"**
>
> I had to be really subservient to try and prevent my father from blowing his top. This was the norm.

> **"**
>
> My mother is a very dominant person. She controls everyone and has no warmth or love.

> **"**
>
> I felt that my older brother was more successful than me and I tried to imitate him to win [my parents'] praise.

Sexual Abuse

This is a subject that needs a special section. Like any experience, it doesn't necessarily lead to SA, but it can definitely be a cause. One thing I've noticed about it, looking in from the outside, is that just one instance can affect the child for a lifetime. Take the case of T, an immature 14-year-old girl, who had recently moved out to the country with her parents. She was settling down well and had several friends when it transpired that she had been sexually abused 'just' once by a music teacher. The family moved straight back to the town they came from and waited for the trial, in which T had to recall that awful time in order to testify.

As her mother says: *"That man was found guilty and sentenced to two years [in prison]; T has a life sentence. She is scared of men now [seven years later] and anyone who tries to get too close to her is given the cold shoulder. So she is still suffering and he got two years. I don't call that justice I'm afraid."*

T's mother was sexually abused many times as a child. Since the episode with her daughter, she carries an enormous weight of guilt due to her inability to protect her daughter, even though she did the best she could. Both T and her mother suffer from SA.

Physical Abuse

This is another habit I haven't experienced. I'm not averse to smacking young children on the bottom, and neither were my parents, but that was as far as it went.

Well, I was hit as a child, not just smacks on the bottom but clouts to the head. It wasn't often, once every couple of months my father would get into a huge rage and one of us (his three children) would end up getting a beating (by this I mean 3 or 4 hits to the head or other part of the body). Unfortunately this had an awful effect on me. I lost all trust in either of my parents, my father because I never knew when he would snap and over what (once the handle of my wardrobe came off in my hand, I was 5, he hit me 4 times round the head and I was sent to bed without dinner, another time I wrote over the wall paper in crayon and he just laughed it off), and my mother for not taking me away from this man who scared me so. She would often threaten us with telling him we'd been naughty, this of course translated into a threat to get him to hit us, or at least in my young mind telling Dad=getting hit.

It is also with some irony I ponder the fact that my mother used to make a point of telling people how wonderful her own father was and that he never hit her (neither of her parents did). As a child I couldn't understand why she stayed with him (he had many other problems) and caused her children to have the childhood they had, but now, at 23, I can see it from her side and can understand how trapped she was, at 7 it's never quite as clear.

I went through a long period of hating my father for what he was doing to my mother (emotionally, he never hit my mum) but not really over the fear he injected into my childhood. I think I was too sensitive as a child but it utterly destroyed my ability to have any fun or try anything out, for fear of being punished.

Even now I have problems trusting people, or believing that I am worthy of something (again related to being hit, it tells you you are worthless) or someone. I know there are many many worse things and I was lucky to have a roof over my head but it still hurts, especially as my mother likes to tell people that I'm a drama queen because I once got upset about it in front of her parents.

41

I love my parents but my relationship with my father, though I no longer hate him, I understand he was ill and he came from a bad place, is completely beyond repair. I feel guilty for telling people about this but I know it's part of my problems now, as an adult.

Psychological Abuse

For me my SA probably began from living with an abusive alcoholic and getting put-downs all the time no matter what I did.

[My mother was] overprotective and always making me feel like a twat when I was a kid, always shouting and telling me I'm wrong especially in front of others.

Criticism from my mum, which I now know stems from her worry of what others will think and how we will be portrayed.

My mum made me feel stupid and she lowered my self-confidence. I felt as if that was how I would always be, that I could never change.

> 66
>
> I learned a 'role' to play. My 'self' wasn't good enough, so I had to find a 'pretend me' that fit in with my household and that carried on out into the rest of the world.

Any form of abuse, in my opinion, changes the way children see themselves and the world. They look inside themselves for reasons why they have been treated in this way, concluding that they must be inherently bad. Their anger towards the abuser or abusers expands to include some or all other people. As adults they feel both undeserving of outside attention and angry with themselves and everyone else, and so they cut themselves off, as much as possible, from the outside world.

That doesn't make them happy, though. It just perpetuates their notion that they are inferior.

Misguided Parenting

Most parents want the best for their children. They bring up their children in a way that they believe is good for them. Parenting is not an inborn quality, but rather something that should be learned. But how many parents attend a parenting course? Can techniques taught in a course apply to every individual child? Which of the many parenting styles taught in courses is the right one to adopt?

Parents can cause a lot of damage to their children without ever knowing it. They can be too dominant, too strict, too lenient or too protective. Over-protective parents, for instance, can foster SA by carrying out tasks that the children are afraid to do themselves. This encourages avoidance, which in turn (as we have seen) raises anxiety.

43

Learned Behaviour

I think my parents kept more secrets than most people. It was convenient for them to live in this way. They wanted to keep up appearances in all sorts of ways. I'm sure they didn't realise what effect this could have on a child growing up in such an atmosphere. If I was told off for saying something 'wrong', I was sure I had committed a heinous crime. I know now that it wouldn't have been so bad to tell any of those secrets, but I didn't understand that at the time. So I kept quiet in order not to 'spill the beans'.

Everyone has things they don't want to tell to the whole world. To this day, I don't know how to deal with these things. I don't know how to avoid saying them without showing obvious embarrassment and confusion.

This is one type of behaviour I learned at home. But usually when we talk about learned behaviour we mean behaviour copied from one or both parents, and this is common amongst SAers. We can point to a parent who showed attributes of SA that we probably learned just by living with them.

> Re: Nature vs. Nurture. For me it was more nurture. I was adopted and had a pretty strict religious type upbringing. My birth parents aren't shy at all ....

Looking back, I now wonder if I had some form of SA when I was younger. I was adopted as a baby. Throughout my childhood and teenage years, I felt as though I was constantly under pressure to be on my best behaviour. Everything I said or did was subject to parental scrutiny – and it didn't by any means always measure up to my adoptive parents' exacting standards.

When I went away to university, everything changed. I could do and say what I liked, and I could be spontaneous without fear of parental disapproval. This, I now realise, was the real me. But when I went back home, this new persona had to go into hiding. I didn't dare risk my adoptive parents' disapproval of what I'd become.

When, at the age of 48, I first met my birth family (all utterly delightful and as mad as a box of frogs), for the first time in my entire life I felt completely at ease in the company of relatives.

I think I'm definitely a product of Nature rather than Nurture.

Bullying

We usually think of bullies as being particularly cruel and vicious children, who probably come from dysfunctional homes. Some people think that these children should be taken out of the classroom to protect their victims. But often the bullies are decent children who don't understand what they're doing. Sometimes a whole class may gang up against one susceptible child. And bullies don't have to be children at all, although you'd think that adults would have more sense.

Other Children

> [Bullying] made me feel like I was under constant scrutiny and couldn't do anything without being pilloried. It left me without confidence in myself and wary of others to the point of feeling better off alone.

> I used to get made fun of as kids recognised I was easy to upset and took advantage of it. I learned to completely ignore other kids and just about to control emotional outbursts which kind of solved that.

> I got SA from being bullied at school, I think. It was made worse by moving at age 14 to a new school. I did have friends but I think I always liked being on my own more than the average boy. In teenage years I studied away from home and was somewhat bullied there because I was from the north and most of the students were from the south. I had some friends there but most of them went home at weekends, so I had little opportunity to learn about socialising. I didn't make any friends other than some fellow students who were all male. I didn't know how to go about making friends or girlfriends from the people in the local area.

> I was bullied right the way through school; I was called names, I was picked on, I was rejected and isolated. I suppose it's pretty self-evident how that led to SA; I just came to expect that kind of treatment and gave up trying.

Teachers

When I was 8, my class teacher was an inexperienced 18-year-old. She wanted the children to like her, and so she kept in with them by humiliating the unpopular ones – me and one boy. Being bullied by other children is bad enough, but when the person in authority says something to make the whole class laugh at you, you feel... I don't really know what I felt. I just accepted it as another of those things that always happened to me. But it must have taken its toll.

Being Made to Feel Different

It can happen at home. They might not mean anything much by it. But you 'know' you're not as clever as your brother, or you're so clumsy that you can never do any jobs properly, or you're too thin, or too fat, or just ugly. Maybe they only meant it as a joke or a term of endearment like "Chubby Cheeks". Even before you go to school, you know that you're different from all the others. Unintentionally, you reflect this to the other children and they sense it straight away. You're different and have to be treated in that way.

It might not happen at home. I couldn't wait to start school. I was so much looking forward to being with other children. But they rejected me from the start; they made me feel different, and I unintentionally perpetuated the notion that I was different.

As adults we're allowed to be different, up to a point. As children, anyone who is different is singled out and ostracised or tormented. I endured it for the whole of my childhood by suppressing my feelings and emotions.

I'm still paying for it now.

Trauma

I had a blushing problem for 55 years. I remember it at infant school. Some teacher accused me of impurity with a classmate girl, cos she said I had kissed her. She took me to the front of the class to show everyone my red face, a signal of shame and guilt, so she said. I was only 11 and I didn't know what she was talking about. From that time onwards, I seem to have had phobias of every aspect of that story. Eg being the centre of attention; people looking at me; being accused of something; girls – especially ones I really liked; figures of authority; sexual matters; teachers; etc, etc, etc.

It was HELL, and it destroyed me. I made others uncomfortable to be with me, it made others blush, job situations were terrible to deal with because I couldn't avoid going crimson at the slightest provocation, bosses found me uncomfortable to deal with. I dreaded going red and this seemed to bring it on even more. It happened anywhere, everywhere, with anyone, for no apparent reason. All I had to do was dread it happening and it would arrive, other times it would happen when I never dreaded it. It just arrived any time all the time. I would sooner have been born a physical cripple than crippled in that way.

At 18, I discovered alcohol, and from the very first drink I knew it eased the blushing problem. It became my medication, and anywhere I went after that, I drank like an idiot to reach a level where I either didn't blush, or I passed a point where I maybe didn't feel so self-conscious. After 35 years of drink, I was not only a blusher, I was downright destroyed by drink.

I joined a 12-step programme for the alcohol problem, and due to my sharing in public, to big and small meetings, etc, I realised one day that I didn't seem to go so red anymore. I must have got more socially confident and the blushing problem seemed to go. If I ever feel it emerging again, I have associated it with too much strong coffee, and I cut it down. I certainly don't have a dread of blushing now. I am still socially phobic, but seem to be much better now re redness, to the point I don't count it such a prob or such a major worry. It was about 1991, it seemed to go when the alcohol left my life. Prior to that, it was my BIG reason to drink like I did.

I tried hypnosis for it – got nowhere. Psychoanalysis – got nowhere. Relaxation – yoga – got jobs working on my own – I never advanced in any job, even though I was a good worker, I seemed always counted as a no-count for promotion due to this "infantile" activity – I never married – the worse thing was avid chain-smoking. As soon as anyone said "hello" out came the fags. It was a deflection for my thinking and the smoke was like a screen between me and the world. Cigs nearly killed me and kept me broke. Now, I've packed those in, which is another share altogether.

The same commenter later added:

66

However, there had been things which led up to that episode, and if it hadn't been that story, something else would have occurred to draw it all to the fore.

Trauma is said to cause SA. It makes sense, too, but that's all I know about it.

Drugs and Alcohol

Alcohol, and drugs even more so, can change your thoughts.

As SA is all about having the wrong thoughts, taking drugs and alcohol can *cause* SA. *They can make you have doubts about yourself that you never had before.* I know this because people have written about it.

If you have never agreed before with any reason you've heard against taking drugs or excessive drinking, think about this one. Unlike the other causes of SA, substance abuse is something you cause yourself, and no one wants to catch SA.

> **"**
>
> I did them [drugs] when I was sixteen – ecstasy, acid, weed, speed. It shames me to think of it.
>
> But the bottom line is: my SA started to surface when I was 17 and I carried on taking drugs until I was 18. I only stopped because I got SA so bad that I stopped going out and the opportunities to take drugs diminished – that is the one good thing that I credit to my SA. Actually, when you think about it, it's quite good.
>
> I used to be full of ideas and a bit mad and always outgoing but now I just have all the symptoms of SA and feel like a sad twat and have no close friends.
>
> It can't have all been the drugs' fault although tripping on acid totally f**ked my head up for a month. I still think drugs played a huge part though. I've recently made the decision to never smoke weed again after a bad experience recently. I was with what used to be my best friend and all of his new friends and I couldn't say a word and nearly exploded.
>
> It was really bad and has knocked me back a bit, which is a shame because it took a lot of guts to go out in the first place.

" I've suffered from SA since early teens (34 now). In response to coping with difficult emotions of SA I started drinking to cope with the feelings, also to cope with the 'boredom' and isolation of my SA. My experience was that the drinking increased my anxiety, depression and exacerbated the SA! My drinking also made me unmotivated to make any changes or deal with my SA, and as a result I feel I have wasted a number of years in my life. In accepting and dealing with my depression and SA I know personally that drinking doesn't have a place in my life.

All the above sounds good, sensible and sound. But alcohol can calm you down and help you to relax. Taken in moderation, it can bring out the personality of an SAer who never shows their true self when sober. SAers, like everyone else, have to realise when they're over the top. When they find themselves taking a few before every social occasion ("just to calm the nerves") or waking up on the floor (and worse), they have to make a decision to stop. When the help becomes a hindrance, you're better off without it.

And, by the way, I've heard that smoking and an excess of caffeine also increase anxiety.

Modern Society

SA festers more easily in modern society. We are better able to escape company. We can communicate with anonymous people who exist, to us, only inside our electronic devices. We can order food, clothes, books and more without ever talking to or seeing another person. If we do go out to buy food, we tend to buy it in an impersonal supermarket rather than the village store where we're more likely to be drawn into conversation.

Politically Correct concepts dictate acceptance of those who are different. But paradoxically, somehow that very attempt to prove adherence to Political Correctness often means that people who are different are avoided, because it's not considered politically correct to draw attention to them or their differences. And despite the emergence of PCness, tabloids in particular cause amusement by shaming others.

Modern work practices relate more to teamwork, seen (for example) in the open-plan office. Employees are expected to be all-rounders, able to …. But I'm jumping the gun.

Decisions

No matter what unfortunate experiences we encountered as children, all of us made decisions about how to behave in order to stop or minimise those experiences. We might remember those decisions clearly. We might not remember them at all; they might have been made so early on that we have no recollection of them. But we made them because we wanted to survive and be loved, and because we wanted to avoid pain.

Those decisions were based on experiences that no longer exist. The behaviours they generated are now old and no longer needed. They should be retired from active service. But they're so ingrained that they won't go quietly. They do their best to hold on to us and keep restraining us.

What Non-SAers Think of the Origins of SA

I don't know how common this view is, but I've heard it: *Why can't you forget what happened and move on?* My response follows.

You can't ignore things that shaped you into the person you have become. You can choose not to talk about them, but they will always be there, inside you.

If you try to keep those things to yourself, you will have less to talk about, because a big part of you will be buried along with those experiences. When someone mentions childhood experiences, you won't be able to join in with yours.

Talking about misfortunes, with yourself or with others, can help to make sense of them. Sometimes it can reduce their significance in your mind, so that being able to talk about them is a way of moving on.

The telling of misfortunate experiences teaches others what can happen, hopefully lessening the likelihood of such events occurring again to other children. It can help to clear up misconceptions about SAers and help people to realise how common SA is.

If bullying is part of the experiences, talking about it teaches about the possible result of bullying. It's all too easy to think that childhood bullying, hard as it is for the victim, has no consequences in adulthood.

Moving on shouldn't come from forgetting, but rather through learning from experiences. I don't write about the past to perpetuate some feeling of victimhood. I'm not stuck in the past. Understanding the past can bring hope for the future. Not understanding can perpetuate learned behaviours from childhood.

Chapter 5

Symptoms of SA

Anxiety leads to certain symptoms, some of which can be noticed by others. SAers tend to see these symptoms as causes of their SA. They think that if only they could solve a particular symptom, their SA would disappear. But focusing on such a goal usually makes the symptom worse.

The solution, the experts say, is to accept that the symptom happens but decide that it is not important. As the attention to the symptom subsides, the symptom itself subsides.

Believing in the insignificance of the symptom is the difficult part, especially when other people react to it.

What you See

Even if you don't see them, we think you see them:
- ☼ Blushing
- ☼ Perspiring
- ☼ Trembling
- ☼ Fearful eyes
- ☼ Avoidance of eye contact
- ☼ Smiling (or not smiling)
- ☼ Awkward body language
- ☼ Panic attacks

These signs don't necessarily point to SA, and not all SAers do all or any of these things.

Blushing

I first became aware of my blushing in early high school I think. I was SA way before that though. In high school it really hit home though, and I was acutely aware of my blushing, and as it was school, others were delighted to point out when someone blushed, which made it far worse. SA meant I shunned being the centre of attention, and blushing meant I shrank back and withdrew all the more. It's such an obvious giveaway to the anxiety within that there was no way I could bluff my way through anxious situations.

My irrational fear of the blush became as strong if not stronger than my irrational fear of social interaction. Put those two factors together and you have a potent mix, and an extremely debilitating one at that. People who don't blush have a hard time understanding, but people who don't have SA have a hard time understanding that too. To me the blushing was the dreaded manifestation of my anxiety and was a beacon for all the world to see and comment on. The combination of these two factors stopped me doing virtually everything in life that I really wanted to do. Don't get me wrong, I still had a life, but as far as building a career and a future for myself was concerned it was a non-starter. It took me till I was 39 before I managed to start doing stuff others do when they leave school.

I considered ETS surgery to end my blushing, but this is risky and has potential permanent side effects which can be as bad as the original problem. This was preferable to suicide though, and that was the point I'd arrived at at that time. In the end I had (more) counselling and employed my own amateur brand of Cognitive Behaviour Therapy: mainly a long process of changing my perception of my blushing and making the problem smaller in my mind so that now it hardly matters.... I still blush now and again, but it doesn't last long and I don't care about it half as much, so the blush dies a quick death. Blushing used to rule my entire life, and that is no exaggeration.

Blushing is the symptom most frequently cited by SAers as the worst part of SA. They have described it as "devastating", or something that "totally ruined my life". Why? Because it rapidly spirals out of control. Something or someone causes you to feel embarrassed. You blush and feel hot. You're sure everyone can see you blushing and they all regard you as immature for behaving in this way. Perhaps they also think you are lying, or at least are hiding something. So you blush a deeper red, while sweat pours off you.

If you're unlucky, people will have noticed your discomfort by now, but there's no escape. It continues to get worse, and you have to stick it out until you're finally released.

SAers generally give blushing a lot more importance than it deserves. Often others don't even notice any blushing even though the SAer felt their cheeks getting hot. Blaming blushing for the discomfort or strange treatment by others can hide the real reason.

Perspiring

66

A couple of weeks ago at work, I was working with 2 blokes and a third one who always embarrasses me walked towards me. Immediately the panic set in and my face and neck were becoming very hot. Sure enough the conversation was directly about me, cos I was in the process of changing jobs, and all I could do was try and talk to them and look at them as if I didn't have a care in the world. The truth was I could feel my armpits getting wet and my chest hot and I swear I had sweat literally running down my legs!!

> I get anxious in certain social situations. My biggest problem is that I sweat, and since I'm obese, I mean sweat HEAVILY. The more I sweat, the more I worry about it, the more self-conscious I become, and the more I lose control.
>
> I avoid social situations. If colleagues are going to the pub for a pint, or someone's arranged a night out or a party, I dread it. Just thinking about it in advance (even weeks in advance) can bring me out in a sweat. I'll do everything I can to make excuses why I can't come, and the nearer the date comes, the more anxious and depressed I get whenever I think about it.
>
> See, what might typically happen is that I'll go somewhere and I'll suddenly start worrying that I'm going to be put on the spot with a personal question or that for some reason I'm going to become the centre of attention. And the minute I start worrying, I start to perspire. Then my heart starts beating faster and I'm there squirming in my seat wondering what to do. And the more I worry, the more I sweat, and it's like I'm trapped. Are people noticing? Is the sweat visible? By the time these questions are running round in my head, I'm so anxious, of course it's visible! Then I'm thinking, have they noticed and they're just too nice to say anything? Do they think I'm just weird?

It can be embarrassing when perspiration shows on your clothes, or if you have to shake hands when yours is clammy.

Fearful Eyes

I saw this in someone once. I just asked a simple question, and I saw the fear in their eyes. I expect I do that too, but I'm really not very bothered about the way I look, including my body language. The important part of all these signs is how much they worry us. We usually know that we do these things, but if knowing doesn't worry us unduly, we can live with them.

Eye Miscontact

Looking away from the person I'm talking to helps me to concentrate on what I'm trying to say. With my eyes pointing towards the floor or the wall, but not really focusing on anything, I can forget that look of sympathy or impatience, which slows me down even more, and attempt to put my thoughts into words. But that causes more automatic thoughts: they must think I'm half-baked if I don't look at them while I'm talking.

SAers also worry that they appear shifty and untrustworthy if they don't maintain eye contact. But looking straight at the person's eyes makes them feel uncomfortable.

Smiling

Some of us smile too much. Others hardly smile at all. I can't explain why I smile too much, but I know I do. I usually feel it when the conversation is over. As soon as I relax, I wonder why my mouth isn't relaxed, and then I find it's because it's stretched out to the sides. Sometimes I do notice it during the conversation. So I stop smiling and then I have to think about continuing without smiling, as well as the rest of my body language, all the while wondering what the other person thinks of me, whether I'm making a fool of myself, and so on. No wonder I can't remember the person's name afterwards!

Most SAers don't smile enough or at all. That is also related to tension as well as to depression. Don't think that they don't want to have fun. It's just that SA stops them.

Body Language

You can see the tension in our bodies: in the way we stand or sit, by the fact that we don't know where to put our hands or our feet. We know it's happening, and knowing it makes us more awkward. It's a vicious circle.

Well, my friend, who has SA too, was followed around a shop once, by a woman working there. She kept following him all around the shop and he got so nervous because of it that he left the shop. On another incident the same thing happened, but he was coming out of the store to get some money from me to pay for something, she came out of the store and was mean to him, accusing him of basically trying to steal a product (which he had actually left inside the store), and acting strangely around the store.

Myself, well, today I was followed around a shop by a security guard, and it was making me very anxious. I didn't want to actually buy anything but I ended up buying the nearest thing I saw – a [chocolate bar] – because I was so nervous. The security guard was stood not far in front of me staring at me. It was an awful feeling. I have gathered that because I look anxious, I look shifty and that's why I'm always followed around shops by the security guards. But it really makes me more anxious and act even more oddly!

Panic Attacks

Am I glad these don't happen to me.

People have described getting very hot, having tears streaming down their faces, and having to suck in a lot of air to avoid fainting. Panic attacks aren't peculiar to SAers, but SAers have particular fears about them when they are over:
"What if someone saw me?"
"How will I live this down?"
"What must they be thinking of me?"

What you Hear

Voice quirks

59

👂 Stammering

👂 Non-spontaneity

Voice Quirks

Our voices usually come out too soft, but occasionally they're too loud. People have described their voices as whispering, squeaking, or like Marge Simpson. Sometimes the first word doesn't come out at all. You can imagine how that makes us feel … or can you? I'll try to explain.

I've been wondering about whether I should say what I'm trying to say; whether it's suitable, appropriate, tactful and more; whether I can explain what I really mean or whether I'll just be misunderstood. Eventually I decide to go for it anyway, and the first thing that happens is that the first word is suppressed altogether.

That, along with a voice that sounds tense, hesitant, strange and not like mine ought to sound, and the looks from the other person showing surprise, compassion or impatience, is constantly on my mind as I attempt to explain whatever it was I wanted to say in the first place. Now what was that?

Stammering

Some SAers stammer, but remember: not all who stammer have SA. As with all these signs, it's not the fact that they happen that is important, but rather how much it bothers us.

Non-Spontaneity

▶
  I plan to be spontaneous tomorrow.

I remember being spontaneous – I really do. Now, I can only be spontaneous when I'm angry. I don't want to be angry, but anger can get me something I can't achieve without it: people listen to me, while usually I'm just ignored. When I'm not angry, it's those thoughts again that block the spontaneity. Constant worrying about what others think of me simply isn't compatible with spontaneity.

> **Lost: spontaneity**
>
> In about 1968 in London.
>
> Anyone who finds it is urged to return it as soon as possible to its owner.
>
> Reward: A big hug and more, to be decided on the spur of the moment.

What you Feel

☼ Tension
☼ Embarrassment
☼ Anger

Tension

It's SA conflict time again. I feel tense and you sense that. I don't initiate a hug because I'm afraid it might not be appropriate or I might not do it right. But you don't initiate it either, because everything about me tells you that I don't want it. Oh but I do. You can't imagine how much I want it.

I can't tell you how frustrating it is. We crave contact with other people. But our body language tells those people that we don't want that contact. And besides, why would anyone want us when they have so many others to choose from?

That's what we think. Often, it seems to me, there has to be some truth in that. Why be with someone who makes you tense (because tension is a bit catching) when you can relax with someone else?

> "
> It's happened to me a few times that friends – even one good friend – broke off the friendship completely because they didn't feel comfortable with me.

Embarrassment

So many things embarrass us: being the centre of attention, being with a group of children, being with someone in authority, forgetting details of previous conversations (because our minds were on other things), receiving and giving compliments and just being with anyone, to name but a few. If you know us, you've felt that embarrassment. Like tension, embarrassment repels the people we yearn to attract.

Anger

Being on the receiving end of our anger is most unusual, and maybe that's why you notice it more. Suddenly, someone you know as quiet, timid and hesitant explodes in a furious flurry of words. Why?

I, too, find it hard to understand. I think it's a result of built-up frustration, mostly with ourselves and sometimes with others for jumping to the wrong conclusions or for ignoring us. I know I do this occasionally. Following the outburst, I can only apologise.

What you Don't See

You don't know what's going on in our minds. Sometimes we

don't know either.

Automatic Thoughts (Fallacies, Delusions)

When walking down the street, do you constantly feel you're being watched?

> **"**
> If there are groups of people around, yes. I was trying to improve my posture and breathing at the suggestion of someone else on the site while on a walk but couldn't stop myself feeling like I was crumpling as I walked past them, as if I was a target for their derision.

> **"**
> I used to, I don't feel it so much now but I still get the anxiety even when the thoughts aren't there.

> **"**
> Yes, people look and stare at me, and people who are with me ask me if I know them. When I say they don't, they ask why they looked at me.

"He doesn't like me." "She thinks I'm stupid." "I'm making a fool of myself." "I'm ugly." "I'm not worthy of them."

These are a few automatic thoughts and they form the basis of half of CBT or Cognitive Behavioural Therapy. As I said before, this isn't a complete guide to treating SA, and I'm not going to give any details about CBT. But it is the most widely-used therapy for SA, and SAers have definitely benefited from it, so I'll explain briefly.

CBT has two parts: cognitive and behavioural. The behavioural part involves doing the things we fear and previously avoided. The cognitive part involves exchanging those automatic thoughts for some more logical ones.

This seems a strange thing to do at first. After all, automatic thoughts appear instinctively. But if you think about the way you might have thought, and practise doing this, eventually the logical thoughts become automatic. There's an example of this in Chapter 6.

Self-Esteem

SAers lack self-esteem in all sorts of areas. For instance:

Our Looks

> 66
>
> I feel I've progressed, but I still have a long way to go especially with relationships. I've never had a boyfriend and at 30 that worries me. I've never had sex either. Once I wanted it, but as time passes it worries me even more and I just put it off. It's connected in some way to my looks which in my opinion turn everyone away, even though people tell me I look good.

That was from someone I have met, so I can testify that she looks fine.

> 66
>
> I was told I was funny looking, ugly and weird and people laughed at me and I haven't been able to shake it off, no matter how hard I try. Deep down, I know I'm not ugly, but when I'm in social situations my mind completely changes and there are those doubts and comments that people have made to me creeping around, and I begin to think I'm the ugliest person there.

Taken to extreme, this sort of illusion is called *body*

dysmorphic disorder. Just as people with anorexia can think that they're fat even though they're thin, good-looking people can think that they're ugly. Of course plenty of people are less good-looking than most of us. But not all of them are self-conscious about their looks. When looks affect a person's actions, when he/she avoids meeting people because of their looks, that's when these thoughts need to be changed.

Our Smells

> **"**
>
> I spend a fortune on perfume and deodorant and worry that I smell bad anyway. It's a horrible thing to experience. I do think the obsession is magnified when I'm anxious. I have asked people to tell me what I smell like a lot as well, and they always say I smell nice but I don't believe it.

SAers really believe things about themselves that simply aren't true. But in reality they are excuses for a lack of social success. Blaming an imagined defect is much easier than admitting that something in our minds is 99% of the problem. Realising this is only the start of the long path towards recovery, but at least it stops us from following the wrong path, trying to solve false problems like imaginary smells.

Our Inability to Socialise

We don't know how to socialise. I'm generalising of course, but I include myself in this. We don't know because we didn't learn how to socialise. And we didn't learn how to socialise because we didn't get a chance to practise. During those very years when we should have been learning this important facility, we were outside the social circle and forced to forfeit that opportunity. So on top of hacking away at our self-esteem, this childhood rejection caused something very real and enduring.

Learning social skills later in life is much more difficult. The knowledge that we don't have those skills makes it extremely difficult to force ourselves to join in where we feel at best tolerated, at worst ridiculed.

The things that most people take for granted just don't come naturally to us, causing questions like:

? When is it appropriate to hug someone you meet?

? What questions are you supposed to ask?

? Which subjects are considered taboo in certain circumstances?

? What can you say in small talk?

? How do you finish the conversation without it seeming as if you're escaping?

It isn't only SAers who identify with these problems, which is why I mentioned the spectrum in Chapter 1.

> "
> Although I wouldn't consider myself to be someone who suffers from SA, I can identify with many of the problems, for example the difficulties in socialising. Often I don't know if I should hug someone, whether or not a hug will be welcome. Small talk at parties can be difficult and knowing when to end a conversation. I worry that people might get bored talking to me for too long.

Feelings and Emotions

Lacking

I would tell my psychologist something that happened to me and he would ask, "How did you feel about that?"

Being asked about my feelings was a new experience for me.

I would rack my brains trying to come up with some emotion or feeling, but I couldn't.

I didn't always have that problem. As a young child I showed emotions just like any other. It was when I started school and found myself the target of teasing that I decided to hide my emotions because I thought (mistakenly) that showing them would cause something worse. That decision led to the following episode:

I was ten years old. Only the girls were in the classroom. One girl said something nasty to one of the others, who burst out crying and ran out of the room. Then, as if I wasn't there, the others decided that they shouldn't treat that girl in that way because it upset her, while it was OK with me because it didn't affect me. I sat and listened in silence, and they carried on believing what they believed.

When you hide your feelings, they don't go away. But they retreat deeper and deeper inside you, so that you know you feel something, but you're not sure what it is. Hiding or internalising your feelings removes a part of you. It makes you seem like a robot. It makes you uninteresting.

When you finally realise the problem and want to change back, you don't know how to. The process begins when you hide your feelings from others, but then they don't seem to have much point, so you lose touch with your own feelings. Fishing them out again is the difficult part.

If only I'd known that when I started with it. But I was only six then.

Invisibility

Tom, Tom the Piper's son
Stole a pig and away did run.
The pig was eat
And Tom was beat,
And Tom went... quietly away and no one noticed his pain.

We don't complain; we don't cry out when we're in pain, or laugh when we're happy. So we're ignored, and then we feel invisible.

"

I feel invisible in all sorts of situations. People don't notice that I exist, they don't relate to me.

For instance, yesterday straight after an exam several students from my course were sitting outside and discussing the exam. When I went out, no one asked me how I found the exam, except for one who is a good friend of mine (the only one on the course). When we walked to the parking area (me and him), we met a girl from the course and she too spoke just to him as if I don't exist.

A few months ago, I went to the wedding of a school friend. I went with a good friend of mine and we met some others from our year at school. They're not friends of either of us, but they were interested in him and not in me. They asked him what he does and so on, but they didn't ask me anything.

When I told my friend how I feel, he laughed at me but he didn't deny that that's what happened. He said it shouldn't bother me.

Even here on the discussion board I often feel that people don't respond to what I write.

Such feelings, which probably have some basis, are obviously caused by us. Our body language makes people believe that we don't want them to relate to us.

But we do. I realise that it's hard to talk to someone who is 'telling' you "*Don't come near me.*" But that's easier than it is for me to change the way I behave. And by making that effort, you could help me (or another SAer) to change.

Jealousy

It's hard not to feel jealous. Other people seem to have it so easy. They go through life just having fun, without a care (or so it seems), while we worry about imagined thoughts, preventing ourselves from having fun and making ourselves unable to be understood. We know we cause all this and that it's all in the mind, and yet it's very real.

Paranoia

If you knew half of what's going on in our minds, you'd think we were paranoid. And you'd be right. Many of us have worked this out for ourselves, but understanding doesn't stop the paranoia. The other person had nothing hurtful in mind when he said what he did; in fact he didn't have anything particular in mind at all. But our first thoughts told us something else, like:

- No one likes me
- Everyone ignores me
- No one is interested in listening to me
- My looks put everyone off
- It would be the end of the world if they realised I have SA / have no friends / have no social life / ....

Like all aspects of SA, paranoia cuts SAers off from everyone else. In his novel *First Light*, Peter Ackroyd compares paranoia to a sheet of ice separating the character from the rest of the world.

Avoidance – the Rapid Spiral

> **"**
> The man who does things makes many mistakes, but he never makes the biggest mistake of all – doing nothing.
>
> *Benjamin Franklin*

> ▶
> **Jackpot Winner Forgoes Prize**
>
> Ms Su Perafraid, winner of 10 million pounds, has lost her right to her prize by failing to claim it. Says Mr Jack Potbringer, a jackpot delivery man, "We even went to 'er 'ouse to give it to 'er. But she didn't open the door. I know she was there though cos I looked through the letter box and saw her cowering there."
>
> *SA Times, some day.*

Let's say you've been invited to a party. You'd like to go because you like to be with people. But you know you'll mess it up. You'll do something silly and people will look at you strangely. Next time they see you they'll know you're a weirdo.

So you don't go. In fact, you keep away from parties altogether. Then you lose contact with your friends because *"They must think I'm strange for not going to parties and they don't need me anyway."*

When people ask you what you do in your free time, you have nothing to say, and you know they think you're weird because you never do anything. So you avoid everyone in the office or the class. Of course attending parties and meeting friends, as well as being fun, is social education. By doing these things people learn how to behave in various situations. If you don't do these things you don't know how to behave, and so the feeling that you behave strangely, which may not have had much basis at the beginning, becomes a reality.

At some point on this journey, you cross the border into SA, but the border is visible only on the map. On the ground, there's no sign of it and you have no idea you crossed it.

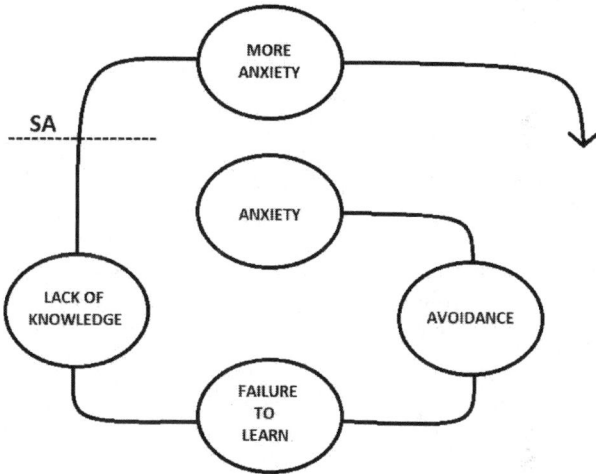

If you continue far enough along this path you eventually become a recluse who is afraid to leave the house even for a short walk, because you are worried about what passers-by will think of you. Some SAers have reached the end of this path, although most have not. The further you go along it, the harder it is to return.

> **How to avoid people** (Some tips from the experts)
>
> **H**ide in a cupboard, behind the sofa, in the garden, loo, kitchen, bedroom, …. anywhere.
>
> **C**heck whether the neighbours' cars have gone before leaving the house
>
> **W**hen walking, make a detour to avoid people.
>
> **P**retend to be asleep.
>
> **D**on't answer the door.
>
> **D**on't answer the phone.
>
> **T**hrow the rubbish out in the middle of the night.

Avoidance is also often caused by a fear of rejection, which probably stems from having been rejected by parents or other children.

Binge Eating

Food provides a way for some SAers to compensate themselves. Really, it just adds to the problems.

I've swung from being underweight to piling on the pounds by starving myself then binge eating so many times I have lost count. I am always on a diet. I have tried every diet going – Atkins, cabbage soup, Carol Vorderman's detox, Rosemary Conley, Slimming World, brown rice and water, fasting, cutting out sugar, cutting out wheat, no dairy, no meat etc, etc. I could go on but it would take up too much space. I mean, I should just eat celery, but I'd get unhappy about myself and end up eating something fatty and sugary to make me feel better. I'm not even classed as overweight, and people tell me I don't look fat, but I FEEL like a big, fat uncontrollable pig. I know I eat for comfort, boredom and other emotional reasons. It's the only comfort I have. I know why I do it, which makes it worse really, but I can't seem to stop. I'm pretty sure my erratic behaviour stems from the emotional distress caused by blushing and SA.

I can't find a regular pattern: sometimes I eat too much, at other times too little or nothing. Sometimes I binge on junk food and then the guilt makes me decide to force-vomit (if you have good abdominals then it's all too easy). Eating badly also makes me feel worse about myself.

Plus I drink way too much. But alcohol doesn't really seem to affect me that much anymore; it still doesn't stop my mind ticking or make me feel relaxed. It helps a bit though.

Thankfully despite all of the above, my excessive nervous tension (both mental and physical) burns enough calories to keep me in good shape.

Serious Consequences

Depression

As I see it, clinical depression comes when you feel that you're in a bad situation and there is no way that that situation can improve. I've never had it. Despite 50-odd years of SA, I've always believed that I can overcome it. I'm not sure whether to call that optimism or madness, but I'm glad of it anyway.

For SAers, depression usually follows avoidance and the subsequent feeling of loneliness. They avoid socialising, fearing that others will think them odd, and then they miss the company of others. The feeling of being lonely and a failure causes depression.

Nearly all SAers suffer, or have suffered, from depression. Anyone who reaches that state should seek professional help to be able to see that their situation is not hopeless. But no professional help should concentrate on depression alone and ignore SA, as so often happens.

Self-Harm

Have you ever self-harmed? (47 votes)	
Yes	28 = 59.57%
No	19 = 40.43%

As someone who can't bear to do anything that causes herself pain, I find self-harm hard to understand, so I'll let others explain.

> ❝
>
> Self-harm (cutting) is a thing I thought I'd never do, cos I didn't 'get' why people did it. I've heard people saying it feels like some sort of release, an adrenaline rush. But still I didn't get why people did this to themselves, leaving scars on their body. Anyway, a few weeks ago I wasn't feeling too good. So I got a scalpel I got from a doctor's a few years ago but never used and just started drawing on my arm. I dunno why I did it, but now I see what those people meant when they said it was like a release, cos I did actually feel better after it, as stoopid as that sounds.

I've been cutting [for about three years] and I still have all the scars running up my arms and legs. Which has messed up any chances of wearing a t-shirt for the next few years, at least. I've only done it a couple of times in the last few months, but can feel it coming back. It's when I get that heat rush through me, when I look in the mirror and my reaction is to want to cut my face apart.

For some reason, though, I wouldn't want to be without it. At least, not until I've lost the need for such a crutch. Scars keep me grounded, they're a way of... hmm, marking my territory, in a way, I guess. So when I don't feel like I belong in my body, that I'm not me, I still have those parts of me that can't be taken away.

It's probably something I should resent in myself, but it's actually something I'm proud of. I don't think I've done anything before that's meant so much to me.

I used to cut myself, more in the past than what I do now (now I hardly do unless I'm feeling really really really c***) mainly my legs and arms. It is kind of a release. I used to do it so I would get scars on me and then people could see that I was hurting, if that makes sense. At school I totally slashed my left hand up, not that anyone there noticed. I did do it for people to notice. But I haven't done it recently.

75

I'm not sure why I do it – I find it very difficult to pin down an exact reason, perhaps it gives me control – I dunno, that sounds dumb, how can you be in control when you're hurting yourself?! But I do know that when you start it can be very addictive and difficult to stop – so don't even bother trying it. I scare myself with it sometimes, it has flashed through my mind on the odd occasion, how easy it would be just to cut, in the right place, just that little bit deeper. Plus I for one certainly don't like my scars!

Anyway, I started self-harming in my early/mid teens and have had 'phases' of it ever since. Hoping this will be my last one.

I suppose I harm myself as a way of proving to myself and others that I really am hurting so much inside and that I am not just making it up. People want me to stop but I like doing it – it makes me feel a bit better.

I don't cut or burn myself, instead when things really get too much for me to cope with I'll be extremely upset, frustrated and completely loathe myself. When this happens the only thing that will make me feel better is to hit my head hard against a wall usually not stopping until I'm bruised and feeling quite drowsy but then at least I feel calm for a while. I often feel like I'm a bad person so feel better to have punished myself. I worried so much that I might do some serious damage. At my worst I was doing this every couple of weeks, but since getting help for my SA 3 months ago and finding this site I haven't felt the urge to do it. Really hoping I never will again.

66

It's ultimately just another form of escapism, a diversion from your problems and yourself (that you hate).

66

For me it's not about being punished: the largest part of it is about stopping the pain by giving yourself a different pain to think about – not unlike hysterical people being slapped. Another part is simply releasing frustration/anger. I have a punch bag which I beat the sh*t out of when I'm angry/ frustrated but it's not the same. The pain is in my head, that's the part that needs to be hit. I think the problem comes when you realise that doing something like that *is* a release. It really works...in the short term. And so the next time you feel like that you do it again, and eventually you just get the urge to self-harm.

66

I like my scars and don't regret them. It reminds me that there were worse times in the past... if that makes sense...

I've done it well over a hundred times on my left arm and wrist – some people have seen my arm and said it is 'disgusting' and that it looks like I have been torturing myself (which I suppose I have). But I don't care. Every time I wake up after I've been pissed and cut myself it's like a fresh start. When the scar heals I heal mentally.

I dunno why self-harm is such a taboo – I'd rather cut myself up than someone else...

> It's a taboo because it isn't a socially acceptable form of escapism: people see the scars and it scares them - it threatens their rose garden view of reality. Drug abuse, self-harm, eating disorders... People always talk about curing these things because people can see them and it offends them. If you hide it, then that's fine. These things are only symptoms of underlying problems: undoubtedly it would be viewed as a good thing if somebody stopped self-harming. But how are they going to express themselves now? Who cares? We can't see it, and now they fit in with our view of how things should be. We are happy.

For yet another reason for staying away from other people, those who self-harm tend to wear clothes that cover up their scars. When the weather's hot this can be annoying, and so they stay at home instead.

Suicide

> ▶ If you think nobody cares if you're alive, try missing a couple of payments.

Here's another poll of SAers:

Have you ever considered committing suicide? (60 votes)	
No, never	9 = 15.00%
It's hard to say whether I have ever seriously considered it but the idea has passed my mind before	18 = 30.00%
Yes, I have gone through periods of seriously considering it	17 = 28.33%

78

Yes and, in fact, I have made an attempt(s) in the past	16 = 26.67%

Suicide may be the ultimate conclusion of depression. If life has become so bad that you can't stand it any longer and you see no possibility of changing it, suicide can seem the logical solution.

I have never considered killing myself, but I see I'm in the minority amongst SAers. I have read posts on discussion boards from people who threaten to commit suicide. Replies mention that things can always get better, and that family members would be devastated. Some say how glad they are that their suicide attempts failed, because things did get better.

Some of the posters remain on the board; some don't. Who knows what happened to them?

Chapter 6

What We Find Hard

For an SAer, life is a struggle. It's embarrassing to admit that things others take for granted are hard for us. Not all of these, of course. We're all different.

Using the Phone

▶

> For the operator press 1. For customer relations press 2. …
> SA sufferers please press 9, where a trained operator will ask
> you questions that require only one-word answers.

The telephone has existed for a long time. It was invented long before any of us were born, and most of us couldn't imagine life without it. And yet there are some SAers who never answer the phone, some who don't make calls, some who don't use it at all.

Why? Because they're afraid of sounding silly, of misunderstanding, of getting tongue-tied. I find that not being able to see the other person's reactions makes phone calls easier than face-to-face conversations, but other SAers find this more difficult. As with anything else, if you avoid using the phone, you become more afraid of it.

A more recent challenge SAers face when using the telephone is being expected to leave a message when no one answers. I still haven't got used to talking to a machine, and I know I sound stupid when I do. The worst feature, I find, is the one that lets you hear your message again before sending it. If I listened to my message, I'd reject it every time, so I just send it. Anyone who knows me knows that I always sound hesitant and that I have a hard time expressing myself orally, so they'll just have to put up with it.

One-to-one Conversations

▶

> Simple Simon met a pieman going to the fair.
> Said Simple Simon to the pieman, "Let me taste your ware."
> Said the pieman to Simple Simon,
> "Erm, do you by any chance have some money?"
> Said Simple Simon to the pieman, "Mmm, that was yummy."

Hesitancy, the result of struggling with self-expression, causes SAers to miss out. It can be much more than a simple case of a pieman losing a pie. An eminently qualified person could miss out on a job by seeming unsure. A relationship might never develop.

One-to-one conversations can be split into several categories:

Small Talk/Strangers

We're all different.

I find small talk fairly easy, especially if I'm talking to a total stranger. The stranger doesn't have any preconceived ideas about me, so treats me like anyone else, and I may never meet that person again, so it doesn't matter what they think of me. But other SAers find all small talk difficult, especially with strangers. Anxiety causes their minds to blank out and they can't think of anything to say. They worry more about what the stranger thinks of them than they do with friends, who know them anyway.

Other problems can arise the second time we meet someone:

I find it hard to remember people I've only met once or even twice. Often I know a name I have heard before but have no idea what they look like which can be problematic when I need to find them. I just have to chance that I'll recognise them again on sight. I seem to remember people better at work by where they sit rather than what they look like. When I am in a new situation I often draw a diagram of who sits where so I can find them again. I actively try to remember features of people's appearance. There's one guy I met who has multiple sclerosis. I remembered him by the features of his disease (difficulty walking, slurred speech), that he was middle-aged and had a beard. You would have thought he should be very distinctive. After I had met him only once, just my luck there was another guy I met soon after at a social event who had difficulty walking, slurred speech, was middle-aged and had a beard and I got him confused embarrassingly. They don't really look alike, I just didn't remember his face at all, only a few key features of him that were unfortunately the same as someone else.

Difficulties in recognising people can be caused by neurological problems rather than by SA. Or they can be a result of those automatic thoughts taking over a large part of the mind. Whatever the cause, such problems can make SA worse because they cause social embarrassment.

Hairdressers

I'm amazed at how often SAers post about visits to hairdressers. It has never occurred to me to be nervous about having my hair cut. But it seems that people are nervous about the conversation they are expected to keep up. The pressure this causes, along with being forced to view themselves in the mirror for the whole session, makes them nervous. Some never pluck up the courage to go to the hairdresser.

Friends

Not all of us have friends. Most of us have fewer friends than we would like. That's because those conversations are so hard.

> 66
>
> I feel like I'm rotten inside – that my very presence is offensive to other people. A colleague at work recently tried to have a conversation with me about books (something she knows I am passionate about) and part of me thought 'Why are you talking to me? Don't do it' and the other part of me felt good. Then I just felt guilty for not being able to show someone who is being nice to me that I appreciate it. I make it so hard for people to get to know me. I can never let anyone in or let my guard down even for a moment. I feel like because I'm feeling horrible I'm causing the other person to feel horrible. When I'm not trying I don't say anything at all but when I'm really trying I can manage a smile and a few words. The trouble is other people don't really see any difference.

> 66
>
> People are very afraid of silence and it makes me feel uncomfortable. I suddenly lose the ability to start a conversation, as if I have nothing to say although I have strong views.

> 66
>
> [I rehearse conversations] because I think it will help me to have answers ready. Funnily enough though, the conversations never go the way I rehearsed them.

"

I usually think a lot. What goes through my head could be described as a loop of recurring thoughts in a panic. I never answer instinctively. I try to make my answers sincere while trying not to hurt the questioner or myself. After a few seconds, I start to think that they think I'm thinking for too long, and so I get under pressure and start to think again and again and again about all the considerations I thought about a second before, without reaching a decision. In the end I choose one of the options at random (not necessarily the one I really want).

I find repeat conversations require you to recall the little social details about other people's lives that you've learned in the initial conversation, for example if someone told me they were going on holiday, or thinking of getting a new car or some problem they've been having. They're all details I could use to start a conversation and keep it going for a while however I never seem to recall those details. Hundreds of such social details about people get fired at you every day. I think it's the stress of a conversation that makes my mind not recall that kind of thing, ie I'm constantly working on my exit strategy/being scared of being boring rather than concentrating on what they're saying. If someone reminds me of the subject it comes back to me, but I don't get the reminder of the right questions to ask up front. There are some embarrassingly large details I forget when under pressure.

A similar problem is I don't remember what I've been doing recently either. What I've been doing is no less interesting than what other people tell me they've been doing but I don't remember it so that's another load of conversation subjects gone. I hate impromptu 'status update' meetings at work. I can never think of what the hell I've been doing all week, what the problems are, what the successes are or anything; much less put it all into a sensible, coherent order under pressure.

I think my social anxiety stems from a pre-knowledge that I've got nothing to say and can't put it into a sensible order. Hence why I go to great lengths to avoid talking to people.

> " When socialising, I am terrified of awkward pauses when I can't think of anything to say. I don't think I have a good social memory. I don't recall on demand all those little details about people's lives that generate small talk. I don't remember that someone's just been on holiday or that they've just bought a new car or whatever. It just doesn't occur to me at the time for some reason so I can't get past the sort of "Hi, how are you doing?" part of the conversation. This means I often feel boring because I can't think of anything to say or worse I say something stupid to fill the space.

Life is a series of choices, some harder to make than others. I often find it harder to make choices than I ought to because, subconsciously, I start to wonder what's expected of me, or what a normal choice might be, or what someone else would like me to choose, rather than simply what I want. I couldn't have said at the time, for instance, why I hesitated so much when someone I was staying with said, "Breakfast will be later; do you want a cup of coffee now?"

Later, I worked out why. It was because I was thinking: *No, I don't want coffee but am I expected to want coffee? Would it be the normal thing to want coffee before breakfast?*

Later still, my thoughts ran on the lines of: *Why would anyone want friends like me when they can have normal friends?*

Boyfriends/Girlfriends

> ▶ SF, quiet and timid, hobbies: getting depressed from loneliness, seeks similar SM to join her.

We're afraid of showing our real selves, of revealing our inner thoughts, of showing our feelings. So we come across as boring and not exactly an ideal partner. What makes it worse is that we know all that. We know that we won't seem interesting to a potential partner, and so we don't search for one.

> It's hard for me to live with the feeling that I'll never get married or have children. For me it's just a dream, because I don't allow myself to have a partner. I can't even go on a date, mostly because of the way I look, and also because I don't talk much and I feel I completely bore everyone around me.

On some SA websites, where all the members are young and single, they see this problem as practically the only one. They think that, if only they could overcome that hurdle, all their problems would be solved. They don't know what awaits them when they have found that partner.

Partnerships

Some SAers do manage to find partners, and even to live happily together with their partners. This raises other problems, though, especially one that seems to be more prominent for women.

Female SAers' husbands seem to be either outgoing or shy. Each one has their own advantages and disadvantages.

The outgoing husband does all the things his SA wife avoids doing. He makes the phone calls, runs all the errands and earns the money. He does these things with the best of intentions: he sees that his wife finds them difficult and wants to make life easier for her. But that encourages his wife to continue the pattern of avoidance, when she needs to break that pattern in order to conquer her fears. It makes her lonely, bored and upset with herself. It lowers her self-esteem and makes her depressed. In addition, she feels she is unworthy of her husband's love, despite his insistence to the contrary. She feels that she is keeping him at home when he could be out enjoying himself.

The shy husband seems more suited to the SA wife. He is happy to stay at home more, and his wife has no choice but to perform tasks that her husband isn't comfortable doing either. But the wife might still not be completely happy, especially if her SA is a screen masking an outgoing personality. She may crave social contact even though she feels inept at it.

And yes, I know that not all couples are married and some partnerships are same-sex. You're welcome to insert, into the above text, words that suit you.

Authority Figures

From the time of my decision to keep quiet at school, I gradually distanced myself from the teachers, with whom I had previously always been friendly and talkative. That caused me to become afraid of talking to them, feeling as if I wasn't good enough to talk to them. By the end of my school years, when we were expected to be able to converse with the teachers on a more adult level, my fears were the most prominent and seemingly ridiculous.

As we progress in life, we extend our fear of teachers to a fear of all authority figures, including lecturers, bosses, policemen and... job interviewers.

Interviews

▶
Wanted: introvert, quiet person, who enjoys working on their own and doesn't mix with other people.

Have you ever seen such an advertisement for a job? I doubt it. They always want people who are outgoing, sociable and team members, and have good communication skills. When they call you for an interview, the manager is looking for these characteristics.

What if the interviewee is shy and nervous? What if he fails dismally on that dreaded question: "*Tell me something about yourself*"? Or she can't think of any advantages she might have over another candidate?

> **66**
>
> When I went to interviews I honestly spent days running through all the possible dialogues... I can't say it helped much. The reason, of course, is to cover all the options, not to get under pressure, to prepare answers in advance. I searched for all the right answers to every possible question. The main reason for doing that, now that I think about it, is my lack of personality, which I felt then... Because I felt I had no personality, I tried to give answers that would sound good to the other side, and not what I really think, so I felt the need to think about these things in advance.

We do have some fine qualities for jobs. We are generally conscientious and determined to work hard. We tend to be perfectionists and don't regard mediocre work as 'good enough'. We get on with the job and don't waste time gossiping. But interviewers don't see that. They see one terrified individual and wonder how that person could get on with the rest of the team. They don't realise that they have placed heavy stones on us causing us to sink, whereas in the work situation we manage to keep afloat.

That doesn't mean, of course, that we always get along swimmingly...

Working

> I have been sitting all week at work, listening to the lively banter, and hardly saying a word myself unless it's to ask how to do something. I can do this, but any conversation beyond the bland and functional is totally beyond me at the moment. I sit there and get bored rigid because all I'm doing is data inputting. Then I try and open my mouth to join in and feel really anxious and so usually end up shutting it again.

> Had a bad day at work – went to see my line manager today. Apparently I had ink on my face that looked like blood. He was making comments and laughing right at me and I ran off really upset. Then he saw me later and made a comment about whether I was alright today, then added about how red I went etc. (He doesn't know my problems and I don't want to tell him.) It made me feel so bad. I hate work. I don't wanna go in tomorrow. He made me feel twenty times lower than before.

> I didn't want anyone at my work to speak to me ever. I actively avoided interacting with them (this was hard in an open plan) and would sweat and stutter if they spoke to me. In the end I left because they were making such an effort and I felt very guilty for my inability to reciprocate (or want to reciprocate) and because I was being sick before work at the very thought of it. The irony was that I was the best worker in the office, never took coffee breaks or time out to chat so I got double the amount of work done.

> Business meetings are about listening and comprehension and trying to think of intelligent questions to try and look good. For one thing, they're usually long and my concentration lapses when something dull is being discussed, and I start thinking about something else. I'm often too shy to ask questions or for someone to repeat something when I don't get something because I don't want to look an idiot in front of my colleagues. So my understanding can often suffer. Also there's almost always a phase where you're asked to summarise something, for example what you've been doing all week or the status of your project. I can never remember under pressure and can't form a coherent picture on demand. I'm always terrified of being asked that. Another one I hate is where you go to a meeting and you're asked to say something about yourself to put your position into context. I can never think of anything to say about myself.

> Listening to others only makes you feel more alienated, and if you track their conversations then you have to do a lot of planning: they might run into a subject that makes you uncomfortable for some reason. If they then ask you, you might be caught out. So listening to them forces you to put mental effort into planning ahead.
> This is why anxious people find socialising such an enormous drain, and it makes them physically tired.

> I sit quietly and concentrate on trying to disappear. It doesn't really work. If they're talking about work, I usually join in, but if it's about other matters, I don't. If I join in, I feel tense in the sense of "What will they say about what I just said?"

> Everyone looks at me with a strange smile, because they're not used to me talking. Young people ignore me. Older ones encourage me.

Some SAers can't work at all. Others have next to no problem. Those in the middle succeed to varying degrees, some particularly seeking out jobs where they are left on their own a lot. This removes a lot of problems, but leaves the SAer feeling that they are not pushing themselves enough by remaining alone.

The best solutions depend on the individual. SA has to be tackled gradually. Jumping in at the deep end is inadvisable. SAers who aren't ready to work with others are better off working on their own.

Group Situations

Group situations are easier and harder to cope with. They're easier because you're not under pressure to talk for fifty percent of the time, as you are in a one-to-one chat. They're harder because it can be difficult to get a word in, the topic can change before you've managed to have your say about the previous topic, and there are more people listening to you if you do manage to join in. If you don't join in, you feel (if you're an SAer) a failure, an outsider and unwanted.

> I have a hard time dealing with business meetings because I have a hard time summarising a situation on demand. For example I can't just tell you my opinion on something or describe what my company is doing about X or Y. I have to go away and think about it and write it down to make it coherent. I miss a lot of things out and feel empty headed and stupid if I am forced to do anything other than answer factual questions. I get around meeting problems by inviting colleagues to 'defend' me by dealing with the parts of a meeting that I can't handle. My ideal meeting is one where I can be invisible and just listen.

Part of CBT involves writing automatic thought pages, in which you record your automatic thoughts and replace them with some more logical thoughts. Although I don't go into detail about CBT in this book, I thought I'd share one example with you in the table on the next page. The events are real and follow an SA therapy session, but the names have been changed.

Parties usually seem more frightening than groups because there are so many people together. We have to remember that we won't have to talk to all the participants together (unless we have to give a speech) and all conversations will be with one other person or with a small group at the most. Still, anticipation of a party is frightening. The thought of spending the whole time on your own watching all the others having a good time is distressing.

Situation	Automatic Thoughts	Feeling(s)	Corrective Thoughts
Describe event objectively	Record automatic thought(s) that precede the feelings	Indicate the type of feeling: sad, anxious, angry, etc.	Record thought(s) to correct the automatic thoughts
After the course, I went to a café with 3 other women from the course: B, R and F. I found it hard to get into the conversation. When I did speak, I hesitated as usual and when I finished I saw R smiling.	♦ How can they have SA if they talk so much? ♦ They invited me to join them only because they wanted to invite B and I'm taking her home afterwards. ♦ What I have to say doesn't interest them. ♦ It's hard for me to express myself, so they have to make an effort to understand me. ♦ They have a lot to say. I'm just wasting their time. ♦ R feels sorry for me. ♦ R is laughing at me.	Sad Hopeless	♦ I know exactly why they're here. They don't have to be exactly like me to suffer from SA. ♦ The fact is they invited me. It doesn't matter why. ♦ I think it is interesting, and they haven't said otherwise. ♦ They are patient. The effort isn't too much for them. ♦ I smile and R smiles back. That's all. ♦ I can't know what R is thinking, so there's no point in wondering.
At some stage, I noticed I wasn't listening to the conversation.	♦ In any case I'm not needed and am not contributing to the conversation, so there's no point in listening. ♦ I don't have strong views on politics, so there's no reason to listen.	Hopeless	♦ It's important to listen. Otherwise I have no chance of joining in. ♦ If I don't listen I become immersed in depressing thoughts that don't help me.

Talking over Loud Music

Not all SAers have this problem and not all who have this problem have SA, but I believe there's a connection. When a large part of your brain is worrying about what the other person thinks, there's less of it left to concentrate on distinguishing the words from the background noise, whatever it is.

> I also have had this problem for many years. Pubs clubs etc have always been a problem. The best way to describe it is that I am unable to filter out the background music, chit chat from my circle of friends talking. I am inclined to think in my case that it is a perception disorder linked to anxiety. I have had this problem with phones at work in the past. Trying to tune out the office noise, chit chat from what the person on the phone is saying. I would be useless in a call centre. Interestingly I have worked with students with Aspergers, who have similar perception issues. Another issue which adds to my problem is that my voice doesn't seem to project very well amid background noise, I guess I'm either quietly spoken or my voice pitch doesn't carry very well.

Being Watched

Sometimes activities we perform easily on our own become a chore when someone is watching. I find this in particular when typing or performing a task on the computer. I tend to make a lot more mistakes when I am being watched.

In George Orwell's *1984*, the hero is under constant surveillance by 'Big Brother'. The way he felt must be something like the way I feel when I'm being watched: as if someone is waiting to pounce on me if I make a mistake, or at least to criticise me. If I have to hold a book or a sheet of paper up so that someone can read it alongside me, I find my hand shaking. Phone calls become more difficult if someone else is also listening to my end of the conversation.

Non-SAers can't understand it when we say we don't like being watched. One SAer found the courage to explain his fear of being watched to a trainer who came to observe his work. Imagine how he felt when the trainer and the supervisor just laughed at this confession.

Eating

Problems with eating can be debilitating to those who suffer from them.

> **"**
> I don't mind eating on my own but can find it quite uncomfortable eating with people I know. I think that I may appear a messy eater to them and/or I will eat too slow that they will be waiting for me to finish. It is even harder if I am the only person out of everyone who is eating!

> **"**
> I could never eat or drink in front of others at work, so I'd never drink stuff like tea if others were about and would just go for a small cup of water or something. Foodwise I'd just take a roll or something so didn't have to confront the evil canteen situation. Only way I can manage to really do it is if I've had something to calm me down and not think about it. Think it stems from me generally not liking a lot of food so used to think I was weird eating what I did.

> **"**
> Last year, at the dreaded Christmas lunch, one of the young part-time staff sitting all the way at the far end of the table, yelled across the room "Is something wrong? You look totally out of it." I could have strangled her. All eyes turned towards me and I just tried to smile and offered up some lame excuse about feeling sick from having eaten too much while I turned bright red and broke into an immediate sweat. (It didn't feel the right time to initiate an awareness-raising seminar on social phobia and its many manifestations.)

Sex

If you haven't had sex by the time you reach a certain age,

whenever it is, you might think that you'll never have the chance to experience it, especially if it is SA that has stopped you from having sex up to now.

Learning to Drive

Learning to drive is another activity that SAers fear. They feel uncomfortable being on their own with the instructor, they worry about doing something wrong, and most of all they worry about the test.

If you're wondering: yes, I do drive, but I left my first instructor because he was too critical.

Giving a Presentation or a Speech

It's hard to explain this. It has something to do with being an extrovert wrapped in SA clothing. But I really enjoy giving presentations or speeches, providing that I have planned them sufficiently well in advance. I enjoy being the centre of attention with all eyes on me.

Most SAers are not like that, and dread having to do anything in front of an audience.

Multitasking (or Doing Several Things at Once)

Receptionists are expected to talk to clients while keeping a phone caller on hold and looking up information on the computer. Mothers have to keep toddlers amused while talking to friends. Life in the fast lane involves multitasking, which is particularly difficult for SAers. That's probably because our brains are overloaded as it is. While talking to someone, we're busy thinking about how we're supposed to behave, whether we sound silly, what the other person is thinking and a thousand other thoughts. There is no room left for multitasking.

Relating to the People We Live With

At first appearance, it seems strange that the people you live with (parents, partners or others) know you the least. But, especially if they are parents and only see you in the home environment, they might know you only as a lively, talkative person and not realise that this part of you is hidden from other people. They don't understand why you can't get a job or have a social life, and wouldn't believe you if you told them. That's not the experience of every SAer, but of some.

Some of us haven't found a way to explain. Those who have managed it have been met by varying degrees of understanding.

Parents naturally want their children to be successful in whatever they do. People whose success has been hampered by SA have the added worry that they are a disappointment to their parents.

Handling Compliments

You have to love yourself before you can accept love from others. And you have to know your worth before you can accept compliments from others. If you denigrate yourself, you can't believe the compliment was intended, and so you search for another reason for the compliment. Maybe they're just mocking you, or they're trying to get something out of you. At best, they feel sorry for you and are trying to be nice. If you can't believe the compliment, it's hard to reply to it. So you blush, hesitate and mutter something inaudible.

> 66
>
> I get very embarrassed when someone says I'm good, clever, nice, etc., and I don't know how to reply. My low self-esteem says the opposite.

Giving compliments is also hard. The effort involved in saying it makes it sound forced and unnatural, and can give the impression that we don't really mean what we say. Sometimes giving a compliment can sound worse than not saying anything at all. In that sense, I have practised avoidance.

Handling Criticism

SAers are no more perfect than anyone else. Sometimes we are criticised for our failings. We tend to agree with the criticism, even if it's only partly true or not true at all. Criticism is second nature to us. We continually judge ourselves unfavourably, and so it feels natural to accept it from others. But instead of vowing to improve in the future, we tend to get depressed by it, thinking that improvement is impossible.

Sometimes we are falsely accused, as can happen to anyone. That makes us confused. Our natural reaction is to agree with criticism, and it's hard to gather up enough self-confidence and courage to crush it on the spot. So the false belief will grow stronger.

> **"**
> Many years ago, I had to ask for a loan in a bank. The bank manager accused me of expecting the loan as my right. It was totally untrue and the accusation, together with my inability to refute it, made me so frustrated that I burst out crying. It was so embarrassing.

Getting Help for SA

Very few SAers can solve their problems with no help at all. But asking for help can be one of the most frightening things you ever do.

Depending on where you live and your financial resources, asking for help can initially involve describing your inner feelings and emotions to someone who has little or no experience in handling such problems. Those SAers who have made that effort have received responses ranging from complete understanding to worse than nothing:

> 66
>
> ... once tried to talk to my doctor phrasing it as general anxiety, but didn't do very well at expressing myself, and got some general anti-anxiety advice. Don't know what I was expecting to get, but made an idiot of myself for sure.

It's often helpful to write down in advance everything you want to say. Then anxiety doesn't cause you to forget or become tongue-tied. You can even give the paper to the doctor or counsellor to read.

SAers are often diagnosed as suffering from depression, drug/alcohol abuse, agoraphobia and more. These diagnoses are correct, but if they are caused by SA that isn't treated, or even mentioned, sufferers will never get to the root of their problems.

This is especially true of depression. SA generally causes depression, and it's all too easy to treat the depression without tackling the SA. This can never be good enough, as it will keep the SA at the same level as it always was, with all the accompanying symptoms, avoidances and worries.

Junior SA

The vast majority of SAers graduated to that dubious qualification while at school, an establishment that causes extra hardships for pupils struggling to understand what's going on:

? Why am I different?

? Why can't I behave like others do?

? Why don't they like me?

? Why do I do exactly the things that I know will make them laugh at me?

? Why do they whisper behind my back?

Children are expected to spend all day and every day together: to study together, play together and eat together. What happens to children who find that hard?

SAers have written about hiding at break times, of going off to eat their sandwiches in a corner on their own, of going off for whole days, just so that they wouldn't have to face being at school.

> **"**
>
> From ever since I remember, I didn't have any friends, except for those I shared a room with, and I couldn't understand what on earth the problem was. In primary school I was rejected socially; I was the school nerd. In secondary school I tried to be accepted and to find friends but was unsuccessful...
>
> Parents? Teachers? ... No one penetrated beneath the armour that I built around me.

Secrets and Children

Most people have something to hide, things they don't want everyone to know. Usually they can handle these things. Keeping certain things secret doesn't stop them from being outgoing, talkative people. Children are less equipped to keep secrets while continuing a normal social life.

> "
>
> ... bedwetting

> "
>
> I had a brother who used to hit me and my other siblings, and that was something I didn't speak about outside the family.

Many of the difficulties mentioned in this chapter are felt by non-SAers, too, especially those who are not at the other end of that spectrum from Chapter 1. It's the degree of difficulty that determines the connection between the activity and SA.

Can you live with it, or is it overpowering?

Chapter 7

How We Feel

Some time ago, a Facebook friend updated her status to *Lonely, handicapped prisoner*. That's because she broke her ankle and had been forced to stay at home for six weeks.

"Then you know how I feel all the time," I commented, even though I hadn't broken anything. Why?

I feel lonely because I like company. I've always liked company. Yet mostly, I push that company away because I'm sure it doesn't really want me.

I feel handicapped because I struggle to do things that most people take for granted. The words come out wrong or not at all. My thoughts can't escape my head.

I feel like a prisoner locked inside invisible walls that I built in no time and have been trying to knock down for ever.

Those feelings by no means define the whole of me, but they're feelings I'd rather not have.

Like everyone else, we have moods. Some days we feel happy, other days sad. The overwhelming feelings caused by SA are loneliness, depression, and, of course, anxiety.

Anxiety

Some SAers know that they have always been worriers. They worry about their family, their security and more. It makes sense that this excessive worrying has expanded to include worrying about how they are perceived.
Other SAers are calmer and less concerned with the

tribulations of daily life. I've never thought of myself as an anxious person, and was surprised to discover that a term with the word *anxiety* in it could apply to me. When I thought about it, though, I agreed that social situations cause me to feel anxious.

Anxiety requires effort and drains your energy. It causes tiredness and lethargy. It consumes so much of your resources that you have little left to concentrate on other things. So you forget faces and facts, creating yet another reason for embarrassment.

Loneliness

There are people who like being on their own. They are not lonely; they're happy with their own company. SAers are on their own more than they want to be. Some are happy to spend some of their time alone, but at other times they would like some company.

Some SAers are not alone at all, yet they still feel lonely. They might have a family, work in an office full of people, or even meet friends. And yet, if they examine their feelings, they feel detached from others and unable to get closer to them. Perhaps it's caused by the inability to explain what's going on inside their heads; the fear of ridicule if the truth were known. No one tells their inner thoughts to everyone, but, if you tell them to no one, they form the barrier that separates you from everyone else.

If you spend a lot of time on your own, it's hard to keep yourself occupied, and so you become bored. You might also appear to be a boring person because you don't have any activities to relate.

Depression

I am not referring here to clinical depression, which I mentioned in Chapter 5. I mean the feeling of being depressed, sad and miserable. We don't want to be miserable, but it's hard to keep happy when you're faced with a problem that severely limits your life, but can't be fully understood by those who haven't experienced it.

I am going to leave this chapter before I get too depressed myself.

Chapter 8

What We Want

Friends

Our years at university, we're told, are the best years of our lives. This is the place that's ready-made for socialising, where you're bound to make lots of friends.

Here are some alternative experiences:

> "
> People in my class seemed to be in their own groups from school so I found it just as hard to fit in with them. It was only when I was working over a long time with a project that I felt I was able to even say hello at times with someone from my class.

> "
> I got on well with the people I lived with, but they weren't particularly outgoing or "laddish". I made zero friends or acquaintances in any of my lectures or tutorials. In the end I found the classroom environment made me too anxious to be able to pay attention to what was going on, learning-wise: I just wanted to get out of there. So I quit uni. I have made several attempts to try again, each having the same results. I may try OU [Open University] next.

> [It was] pretty horrible. I tried to make friends, and did succeed in making some quite close friends, but ended up having some major and very emotional fallings-out as well, because I trusted too easily, gave too much, was too honest, and basically didn't have a clue.

At school, at work, at clubs, SAers report being unable to make friends and consequently not having many or having none at all. Most people would probably assume they don't want to have friends. The sad truth is that they do.

Relationships

As hinted earlier, SAers find it hard to form relationships. They might want to get to know a member of the opposite (or same) sex, but their body language and their conversation (or lack of it) say just the opposite: "*Stay away from me. I'm not interested.*"

Why is that? It's because inside they are positive that they don't deserve the relationship; that they are so stupid, ignorant, inept and so on that no one could possibly be attracted to them. Their lack of self-esteem tells potential partners to keep away. This is just another conflict in our lives.

> I'd like to have some girls as friends mainly because I used to actually get on quite well with girls before I cut myself off from most people, but I can't imagine having a relationship. Until I went to a [meeting of SAers] this year, I hadn't spoken to a girl my age for more than five years, so I think I'd find it very hard to be in a relationship now anyway. Just being able to speak without being so nervous and thinking I'm so ugly would make me happy.

> It's hard to explain why men frighten me. I don't know how to love and be loved because I didn't receive any affection as a child.

To Relax

We'll try anything to break the tension you feel around us: meditation, yoga, alcohol, drugs, medicines, hypnosis and good old psychotherapy. Personally I've hardly done any of those, because I don't believe in them. But being able to relax in company is what we all yearn for, and what usually seems unattainable.

Happiness

> ▶ You are about to enter to a new life, called *happiness*.
> You are not allowed to take any baggage with you.

Some SAers have no hope for the future. They are the ones who are constantly depressed and think about suicide. The rest of us are dreamers. We believe the future holds a better life. Some of us even believe that we will achieve happiness one day.

When I was at school, I dreamed of being involved in an accident and being confined to a wheelchair and helped around the school by all the other girls, who would suddenly become nice and friendly towards me. I didn't really think it would be nice to be disabled (even temporarily), but I imagined it solving all my problems.

Nowadays, I am truly happy and blessed with a loving family and a comfortable life. I still wish SA didn't plague me, but I'm not doing too badly all-in-all. I know I could be happier if SA didn't stop me, albeit partially, from communicating, but I can't realistically expect it to retreat enough for that, especially after a lifetime of struggling against it and often giving in to it.

I am optimistic, though, and believe I can continue to make progress and achieve further happiness. I know that my success depends entirely on me... with a little help from my friends.

Chapter 9

What Helps

The people I have described in this book are unhappy with their lives to a greater or lesser extent. On top of that, many very intelligent people are unable to work and are living off taxpayers – not because they're lazy, but because of a very real disability, and I hope that after reading this book you agree about that. There has to be a way of helping those people to get back to work, as well as facilitating their participation in other aspects of life. But what is it?

Therapy

The main feature of SA is false thinking. So any therapy that works has to change those false thoughts. Another essential outcome of therapy is a change in behaviour to stop the avoidance pattern, as well as to acquire those social skills we 'forgot' to pick up on the way to becoming an adult.

CBT (Cognitive Behavioural Therapy), which I've mentioned before in this book, is generally considered to be the most effective therapy for SA.

Other types of therapy include hypnotherapy, psychotherapy, biofeedback (in which psychologists help tense and anxious clients to relax by using signals from their own bodies) and neuro-linguistic processing (which uses vivid mental imagery to change the way we think about things).

What works best probably depends on the person. Some people need to return to their past to dig up buried emotions or to pick up from where their path was diverted. Others don't find any purpose in going back, preferring to work on their current thoughts and behaviour.

I have to say, I only partly agree with what I wrote above: '*The main feature of SA is false thinking.*' This is the view of CBT therapists. I think false thinking is usually what plants the original SA seed. But once SA has developed and grown into a fully-fledged organism, it works on SAers' behaviour and really does make them weird in the eyes of non-SAers.

Internet and Online Forums

The Internet has made an enormous difference to SAers. People who had no outlet for their feelings have been able to pour them out to anonymous beings somewhere in the world. Many people have written or 'chatted' to others on the net. Why is it particularly significant for SAers? I can only speak from my experience and let others speak of theirs. Writing on a computer allows me to compose my thoughts without the pressure of having another person in the vicinity. It gives me as much time as I need to think what I want to say and express those thoughts coherently. And yet it's immediate. When I press the *Send* button, someone at the end of a lot of wires and other communication devices receives my words. It's the nearest I can get to spontaneity.

When I write online, I feel as good as anyone else. When I chat face-to-face, I always feel at a disadvantage – that everyone else is better at it than I am.

Writing on the Internet has brought out a feeling I hardly noticed, teaching me a lot about myself. Usually, when I start writing, I think I have nothing to say, but then the words just flow out. I imagine that this is what talking ought to be like. I seem to remember that it was like that once …

> Chat: a wonderful invention for SAers. Where else can you feel like one of the crowd? Where else can you express yourself without exposing yourself? I was hooked on chat. I'd spend hours at it. All my evenings were devoted to it. We formed a group, and I was popular there. Actually it depressed me that my popularity couldn't continue in real life. After some time it all broke up, and then I got fed up with chat. Since then I've kept away from it.

There are many forums on the net specifically for SAers around the world. I remember well the jubilation, probably felt by every SAer who comes upon a forum or an explanation of SA, that I felt on discovering that there are others – many others – who have similar feelings to mine.

Unfortunately, as we get used to this knowledge, the jubilation subsides. It's still nice to be aware that we're not alone, but that awareness doesn't tame SA. Nothing can tame SA but hard work, determination, and belief that it can be done.

So, what do we get out of SA forums? These are some of the points that have been mentioned on forums:

- ☺ To know I exist.
- ☺ I have nowhere else to go.
- ☺ I feel comfortable here.
- ☺ Without this place I don't think I'd be able to say a word to anyone, on or offline, at all.
- ☺ People here are like me.
- ☺ Before, I thought I was alone.
- ☺ To get and give advice.

☺ It's just nice to hear from people who can relate to what I go through. There's no other site where I can read something and say, "Oh my God...I do that!"

☺ To escape from the Hell in which I live and the people who have trapped me here.

☺ It's comforting to know there are others like me.

☺ It's comforting to know others can understand me.

☺ The site has shown me how fortunate I've been.

In addition, SA forums enable us to share information about the different ways of dealing with SA.

Posting on a forum helps SAers to cross one bridge – one of the many we have to cross on the path to recovery. Some lurk on a discussion board for a long time before plucking up the courage to post. The first post is usually very nerve-racking and wakens many fears: *Will they understand it? Will they relate to it? Will anyone reply to it? Will they reply in a friendly way, or will they tear it to shreds?*

As we post more, those fears diminish and dissolve into calmer thoughts: *I've written my bit; it'll be nice if someone replies, but if they don't, who cares? Some people might not agree with what I wrote, but that's OK because we're all different.*

Sometimes we jump to the wrong conclusions. When someone complains that other posters are too cliquey, or too attacking, half of us think that we were at fault. We can see a disagreement as a personal attack. If some feature doesn't work on the site, we might think we were purposely barred from using that feature as a punishment for something we did but don't know about. SAers have been known to complain that their thread was deleted, while in fact it's still there but on a previous page, newer posts having replaced theirs on the top page.

Belonging to a forum can also help with that paranoid assumption: *If someone finds out that I post on this board, they'll write me off as a nutcase.* Getting over that feeling can be a long process. Some SAers don't last the course. They remain so scared that they might be discovered that not only do they disconnect themselves from the group of people who can provide understanding and support, but in some cases they go to great lengths to cover up all their traces.

One word of caution: while most people on SA forums are nice, kind and understanding, the forums are open to everyone and there will always be a few spiteful people who take advantage of that open-door freedom to attack, hurt, insult, offend and otherwise distress vulnerable members of the forum. For this reason it's best to find a forum that's moderated, because in such a forum offenders can be banned from posting.

Meetings

SA forums provide a convenient way of getting SAers together. Many are too afraid to get to this step, but, for those who do, the experience is generally positive. Meetings can be as a group or one-to-one. Some meetings have even led to partnerships.

> 66
>
> I have met people from the forum, and it's much easier to open up to people who know. My main difficulty is: "What will they say about me when they find out I have SA?", and in a meeting like that everything's open. They know who you are.

Meeting up can be hard, though, and requires some bravery and staying power. Depending on the people, two SAers sitting together can struggle to keep up a conversation, despite having so much in common. Even SAers who are

114

verbose in an online forum can be very quiet in actual, face-to-face meetings. It can be helpful to plan topics for conversation in advance.

Self-Help Groups

As with all self-help groups, members have had good and bad experiences. Meeting people with similar problems can be uplifting. It can be easier to open up when you feel that you can be understood. And the group can support you and help to practise being in unfamiliar situations. Unfortunately, sometimes a self-help group can be disrupted by certain members, especially if they don't really belong in the group.

Medicinal Drugs

Various medicines are prescribed for anxiety. They don't provide any cure on their own, but they can reduce anxiety enough to enable SAers to push themselves to do things they wouldn't have done without the medicine. This must be useful, as it shows SAers that they can do these things and also provides experience, which in turn helps them discover how to behave in these situations and also gives them topics for conversation. Many SAers praise the benefits of taking medicines.

But medicines can have unfortunate side-effects, and they don't work in the same way for every person. Withdrawal symptoms can occur if you try to come off them. For these reasons, I decided not to start taking them. I didn't want to run the risk of increasing my problems.

DIY

Some people have combated SA on their own. By reading and following books and other information, including those listed at the end of this book, they have prevailed over SA and succeeded in transforming their lives into happy and fulfilling ones.

Self-therapy requires very strong motivation and will. Let's face it: most people can't even stick to a diet, let alone revolutionise their thoughts and the behaviour patterns learnt over many years.

Chapter 10

Advantages to Having SA???????

This is a very short chapter. You may be wondering why it's here at all.

But it's true that having SA can affect a person's personality in a positive way. It can make them more sympathetic to the problems of others.

We're always too hard on ourselves, and chastise ourselves over the 'mistakes' we make in life. But when we see the same or other problematic behaviour in others, our experiences make us more understanding and accepting of it.

Next chapter …

Chapter 11

Solving The Problem

Is It Really SA?

The first stage in solving a problem is to analyse it. If you want to solve your own or someone else's social anxiety, you have to make sure that they really have SA.

There are various tests for SA, the most famous of which is the Liebowitz Social Anxiety Scale. I have decided that this test doesn't work for me, because it assumes that talking to strangers is harder than talking to friends, and that giving a presentation is harder than having a one-to-one conversation. Other tests, with a larger number of questions, can give different results. I would advise, instead of these tests, deciding whether the person fits a description of SA, or whether they empathise with feelings expressed by SAers on SA discussion boards or in personal stories.

The next stage is to get a professional assessment.

What SAers Have to Do

For several years, I used to think my aim was to get rid of SA – to remove it totally from my system.

I no longer believe that. I've come to the conclusion that SA never completely goes away. SA isn't alone in this. Consider this quote (about smoking):

> Thus began a love affair which was to continue for the next twenty years and that still tries to lure me into its poisonous rapture eight years after the last puff left my lungs.
>
> **From 'From Zaftig to Aspie' by DJ Kirby**

I've never smoked, but I think the feeling described is pretty normal. People who enjoy smoking don't usually grow to hate cigarettes after they give up the habit. Their craving is always there in the background. In fact, when I contacted DJ about using her quote in this book, she said, "I still crave cigarettes seventeen years on!"

Take stammering, too. The British Stammering Association (https://www.stammering.org/) has this to say about so-called cures:

> …while there are techniques which can be extremely helpful, these require ongoing practice to become effective. This is not the same as a 'cure' - which implies something administered by an expert which will work for everyone in all situations. People who claim to have found a cure for stammering often passionately believe they have something to offer. We do not suggest that their motives are anything other than genuine, but we believe these claims are misleading. BSA advises caution in respect of such courses and we do not publicise them in our literature or on our website.

Note the term *"ongoing practice"*. In other words, the tendency to stammer never goes away, but use of the techniques helps to keep it hidden.

In the same way, SA is always there, in the background, threatening to disrupt our lives. But we don't have to feel depressed by this. In fact, understanding it this way can make things easier. Instead of struggling with an impossible aim, we can work to gradually reduce the negative effects of SA – to make friends with SA.

As I've mentioned before, we have to change our automatic thoughts and learn social behaviour. We also have to do all the things we feel afraid of; not all at once, but gradually, starting with the easier ones and working up to the hardest. We could do with some help with this. In particular...

What Non-SAers Can Do

In a previous draft of this book, I had a list of things not to say to an SAer. It went like this.

Don't Say...

☹ Cheer up it can't be that bad!

☹ Why don't you smile? You have such a pretty smile.

☹ Are you OK? You look bored.

☹ Cheer up, love, it might never happen!

☹ Smile, you're ruining the scenery.

☹ He's so *shy*.

☹ You're QUIET, aren't you?

☹ It speaks!

☹ What did you do during the weekend?

☹ A penny for them.

☹ This is Susan. She doesn't like associating with people.

...Or the Sarcastic Ones

☹ You're full of conversation today.

☹ I can't get a word in edgeways.

☹ You're a bundle of laughs.

Don't Draw Attention to our Symptoms

☹ You're as red as a beetroot.

☹ What's up? You look as if you've seen a ghost.

I don't agree with those any more. While they are all things that people have said, and while they are things that make SAers feel awful, other people can't be expected to remember the list each time they open their mouths. It's much better for them to try to do the positive things and maybe that will automatically diminish the negative. But they don't need to worry that they've made some *faux pas*. I wouldn't want such a list to stop others from talking to me.

Involve Us

☺ Talk to us. It'll be hard for you. We might not answer much. But we want that contact.

You find yourself with 3 other people. They're all joining in the conversation. As usual, you're not, although you do have views on the subject. You're sure they must notice this and you're wondering whether they'll think it rude if you slink away. Then one of them turns to you and says, "Hey, what do you think about that?"

Apart from feelings of panic, what's going through your head? (45 votes)

121

How nice of them to help me to join in. I was wondering whether to say this. Here's my opportunity.	24 = 53.33%
That's so nice of them, but they'll think my views are weird. I'll just say I haven't thought about it.	19 = 42.22%
They're just trying to embarrass me. I wish they'd leave me alone.	2 = 4.44%

☺ Ask us to join you. It might be hard for us to say "No" if that's what we decide to do, but it's better than never being asked:

We often complain that other people say the wrong things, but do we know what we'd like them to say (or not say)?

Here's the scenario (and it doesn't matter if you don't work – just imagine):

You work in an office. At lunchtime a group of people decide to go to lunch together.

Do you want them to invite you to join them?	42 votes
Yes and I'll go with them. Even if I mess it up it's better than staying on my own.	12 = 28.57%
Yes. I'll probably decline, but that's better than being ignored.	24 = 57.14%
No.	6 = 14.29%

Ask but Don't Insist...

...on details of our weekend/holiday/whatever. If we don't

want to say, it's probably because we're embarrassed to say we didn't do anything.

Ask but Don't Patronise

> "
> As recently as a couple of months ago, I had someone put on a 'sympathetic' face and speak to me in a tone of voice that you would use to address a small child or a pet. I am certain that people think I'm a bit backward, mentally defective, not all there, etc.

Just as people in wheelchairs don't like it when others address questions about them to other people, we don't like being treated like small children. I know our external behaviour sometimes resembles that of children, but internally we passed that stage a long time ago.

Listen to Us

SAers are good listeners. You can reel off all your problems to us and we will sympathise, empathise and continue listening much longer than most non-SAers.

But remember that we have problems too, and we want to talk about them even if it seems as if we don't. Hesitation doesn't necessarily imply unwillingness, but it might do. You have to judge when we want to talk but are having difficulty and when we don't and think you are interfering.

I'm sorry to make it hard for you. I promise I don't want to.

Understand...

...that we're making an enormous effort by just being there and trying to do what everyone else does. Please try to help by:

- ☺ filling in the gaps
- ☺ being patient
- ☺ trying not to show that you think we're weird.

What I Think Now

Forget all those 'Don'ts'. Remember the positive ways of helping, and try to match them to what you know of the person you're trying to help. Here are two examples of people who weren't considerate:

> ❝
>
> Recently I was in a group where we did a supposedly self-awareness exercise. Ironically, the exercise was supposed to help us feel positive about ourselves. We had to each write anonymously on slips of paper a few words or sentences about how we saw each individual in the group. The instructions were for positive comments only.
>
> Somewhat hesitantly, I opened my pile of slips from the others in the group. How can summing me up in one single word, such as 'Quiet' or 'Shy' be helpful? Worse still, as one person wrote: 'Quiet, reserved, only talks to individuals when spoken to.' Can anyone really think this is a positive comment? I'm still hurting from this.

While the comments mentioned in the above quote were probably all true, the writer would have been all too aware of having those traits – and certainly wouldn't want to be told of them as supposedly 'positive' comments.

Let me tell you about something that happened to me quite recently. Someone followed me on Twitter and I followed her back, as you do. Then she sent me a message and I replied and she wrote back.

Here's the conversation:

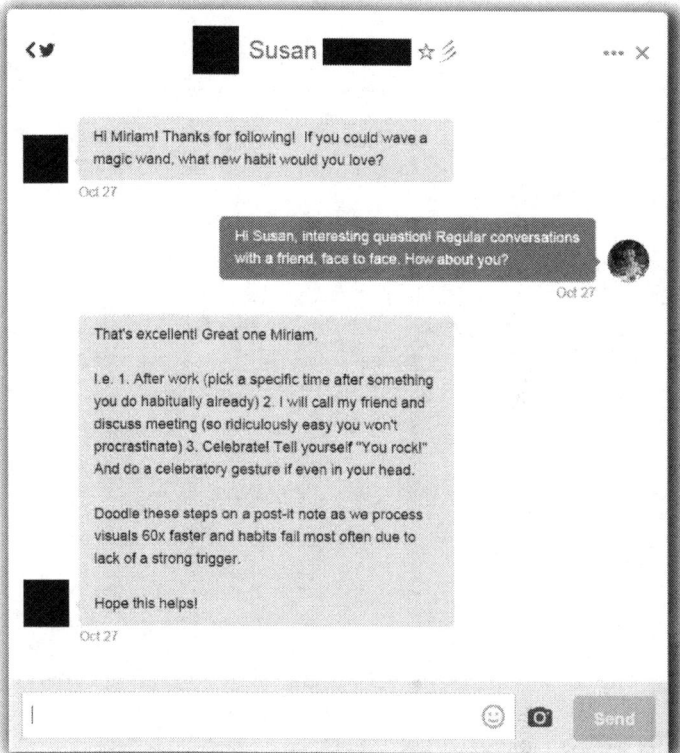

Susan ☆

Hi Miriam! Thanks for following! If you could wave a magic wand, what new habit would you love?

Oct 27

Hi Susan, interesting question! Regular conversations with a friend, face to face. How about you?

Oct 27

That's excellent! Great one Miriam.

I.e. 1. After work (pick a specific time after something you do habitually already) 2. I will call my friend and discuss meeting (so ridiculously easy you won't procrastinate) 3. Celebrate! Tell yourself "You rock!" And do a celebratory gesture if even in your head.

Doodle these steps on a post-it note as we process visuals 60x faster and habits fail most often due to lack of a strong trigger.

Hope this helps!

Oct 27

It *was* an interesting question. I considered my answer carefully. According to her Twitter profile, she lives in Hawaii and is an author, mentor, speaker, entrepreneur and visual thinker. I chose to ignore all that and think of her as a person. She chose to ignore my choice and answer as my mentor. I didn't ask for her advice; she just gave it.

But, Susan from Hawaii, you don't know me, so how do you know whether your advice has any relevance for me? How do you know whether calling a friend to discuss meeting is ridiculously easy for me? Or even whether I have a friend to call? How do you know whether your advice will be useful for me or the opposite – that it'll make me feel like a failure because what for you is ridiculously easy doesn't feel like that for me?

So, thank you, Susan from Hawaii. I know you mean well (and probably want to find new clients) but I'd rather you didn't do that to me.

And to the rest of the non-SA world: Although I can't expect you to follow a long list of rules, I can hope you realise that people don't necessarily want to be the way they are, that human beings differ from each other, and how a seemingly innocent, off-the-cuff remark might affect someone who is not you.

Stopping SA Before it gets Ingrained

> 66
>
> I'm still severely p*ssed off with my school for not being more help. I did basically everything they seemed to want me to, behaved myself, got good grades to push them up the league tables, didn't cause any trouble, kept going despite the hell I was going through thanks to the other pupils, etc. And in return, I get pushed out at the end depressed and unable to cope with adult life.
>
> Seems like if I wanted any sympathy and help I should have got myself involved in drugs and crime and failed all my exams.

Children change their personalities much more easily than adults do. That's why most of us caught SA as children. But it's also why it would have made it much easier for us if we could have dealt with our problems then, before we became set in our ways, and before missed experiences made it difficult to catch up.

The adults in our lives probably didn't notice we had a problem or didn't realise the significance of it. They thought it was something we'd grow out of. They may even have treasured the silence. It's natural for teachers to notice the children who make a noise in the classroom or behave in a violent way. Children who answer the teacher's questions are praised for taking part in the lesson. Children who disrupt the lesson or attack another child are told off and might be sent to therapy. But we, who did neither, just kept quiet – and so the teachers just didn't notice us.

> **"**
>
> I was very quiet in the class. I went to all the lessons. I didn't disrupt the class. So the teachers thought I was alright. If I'd been hyperactive, for instance, they'd have sent me straight to the school counsellor. They just didn't know about SA.

How can that be changed? In my opinion, teachers should be taught that the quiet child needs as much attention as the noisy one. School staff should be much more aware of bullying, which is one of the main factors leading to the development of SA.

Teachers and others involved in education should have specific training in recognising when bullying is occurring and in methods of dealing with it effectively. Anti-bullying policies should be taken very seriously, and their implementation given greater priority. There should be more social education in which, for example, children learn how simple taunting can affect a sensitive child. And quiet children, themselves, should be helped to bring their feelings out into the open, as well as being advised about different ways of behaving.

Breaking Down the Stigma

Times have changed since the days of my youth. If I ever thought about mental illness then, it was in connection with 'mental asylums,' as we used to call them. The people inside those establishments, I believed, were crazy and needed to be locked up.

I know better now. But despite all the changes in perception of mental health issues over the years, stigma still exists and that includes SA, that common and little-known disorder.

If you've read this book and you don't have SA, you're in a good position to join us in fighting this particular stigma. That would help SAers to be more open and seek help for their problems. It would help us bond with those who share common feelings instead of struggling with them alone.

Chapter 12

My Advice

I am not, and have never claimed to be, an expert in social anxiety. My qualifications are unconnected to SA and I have conducted no scientific study of it. However, as someone who has knowingly lived with SA for several years, and who has been in close contact with many others, similarly afflicted, I offer my advice for anyone who is interested. Some of it is scattered throughout this book. I present it here in a more structured format.

One Size Fits All?

There is no single solution. What works for one person might be useless for someone else.

Don't be disheartened by that. Keep trying different ways until you find those that suit you. But don't give up on a plan too soon. If a plan didn't work out, think how it could be improved, break it down into smaller steps.

A mistake is not a sign of failure if you use it as a lesson for the future.

Make Friends with SA

If you've been putting all your energy into getting rid of SA, then stop. You will never get rid of it. But that doesn't have to be a depressing thought. On the contrary: if ridding yourself of SA seemed like a daunting task, making friends with the beast is much easier... well, it's easier, anyway.

"Hey, people have claimed that's exactly what they've done. They say they used to have SA and now they don't. Are you

accusing them of lying?"

No, I'm not. I think they believe what they say. I've met people who made that claim, and yet I can see, hear and feel SA in them. I think what they really mean is that they're able to do things they wouldn't have done previously. They do that by listening to SA, by discussing the challenges with SA, by asserting their authority over SA. But SA is still there; it's just not as powerful as it was.

People say the same things about stammering. It's always there in the background, threatening to show itself. But you know you have the tools to control it.

Work Out Your Own Strategy

Read online. Read books. Plenty of advice is available, but is it all useful? Be wary of anyone who tries to push you in a particular direction, even if they have proof that it worked for them. Only you can decide which advice to follow – which tips will work for you.

However, don't reject a tip out of hand. It might sound impossible for you now, but you can work up to it.

Any plan has to include goals, and steps leading to each goal. Climbing to the roof might seem impossible, but if you tackle each rung at a time, you'll get there in the end.

CBT Might be the Solution

CBT might be all you ever need to tackle SA. You might work at changing your thoughts and your behaviour and decide that's all you need to do.

But what if that doesn't work for you? Instead of trying to swap automatic thoughts for new ones, try to make friends with the thoughts. Talk about them instead of suppressing them. Don't be afraid of them. Don't let them embarrass you. If you express your thoughts, it'll help others to know you. If you don't, you'll remain a closed box, and those adjectives will never leave you. (*Stupid, boring, stuck-up*; you know the ones.)

With Whom?

Are you going to work on SA alone or find help? Are you motivated enough to help yourself? Do you have enough confidence that you can work on it alone? Are you ready to share your inner thoughts with another? Will the other be a friend or a professional?

These are all questions that can help you decide how to proceed.

Homework

These are things you can do at home, on your own:
- Work out who you are, what you believe in, what's important to you, what you enjoy doing. What music, films, books you like. Where you like to go. Write them down, if you like. Memorise them so you have things to talk about – things you won't have to delve down deeply for when put on the spot. Remember, you have as much to say as anyone else, and just as much right to say it.
- Think up questions to ask of others, so that you can show you're interested in them. Because you *are* interested; they just think you're not.
- In particular, think up ways of continuing after the HAY question (How Are You?). You know the one?
  "*How are you?*"
  "*Fine, thanks. How are you?*" – at which point there's nothing else to say and you or they start to

drift away. But really there's plenty to say. The problem is remembering, under pressure, what those things are.

I'm not going to give ideas, because it's very individual, but you need to make a list and memorise it. The items you pick from your list when the time comes will also differ depending on who you're talking to, but start by believing that you have stuff to say and they have stuff to say. You have to tell them about your stuff and ask them about theirs. I'm not saying that's easy, but it will get easier with practice, as long as you've done your homework first. If you don't have your list ready in your mind, you won't be able to make it up as you go – not if you have SA.

- Write a list of responses to those annoying things that some people are bound to say to you – the ones I listed in Chapter 11. For instance, *"You're as red as a beetroot,"* could be answered with, *"I love the colour red. It reminds me of sitting on the beach and watching the sun as it goes down, turning orange and then a deep red."* Or, *"You're quiet." "Yes, I am. I'm listening to you. You were saying...?"*

- Make a list of your normal thoughts during a conversation, eg *They think I'm boring.* Write new thoughts, like *I'm going to make this conversation interesting. Even if I don't have an experience to add, I can ask questions.* Memorise the list. Then the new thoughts might pop into your head during the conversation.

- Talk to yourself. I know that sounds crazy, but when you're out of practice with speaking to others, I believe it helps to get used to the sound of your own voice. Otherwise, when you do speak up, it could surprise you almost as much as it will surprise others. Also, without the anxiety caused by the presence of others, you'll be able to think up topics of conversation and content that you can remember for a real conversation.

- Question what you believe to be true about yourself. Why is this important? Because beliefs are self-fulfilling prophecies. If you believe you will fail at something, the likelihood is that you will fail. For example, say you have to give a presentation. You might believe you'll be so anxious you won't be able to get the words out.

- Make a list of beliefs you would like to hold. For example: *This presentation will go well.* Then decide what you need to do to make those beliefs come true. In the case of the presentation, practise it, over and over. Then, if possible, practise it in front of someone else.

- While we're on the subject of presentations, don't begin with a presentation about SA. In my experience, it's the most frightening, worrying, anxiety-causing type of presentation you can give. But, when you're ready to venture into that topic, it can also be fulfilling, and listeners will be on your side, rooting for you. Well, I can't promise that, of course, but I haven't had any opposition yet. Giving a presentation on SA brings an overwhelming sense of achievement in your accomplishment and also in knowing that you've furthered the cause of raising awareness of SA.

Join an Online SA Forum

The fact that you can see for yourself that you're not alone in feeling as you do, is reason enough to join an online forum. Read what they say. You won't recognise all their feelings and problems, because we're all different. You might discover feelings you didn't even realise you had. You can learn about treatments and find out what worked for others. You can get to know people who generally won't be judgemental, and maybe even meet up with them.

People with SA are much more open in a forum than they

would be face-to-face. They bring up interesting topics that lead to lively discussions.

You can be as anonymous as you like. You can hide behind a made-up name. Nearly everyone needs to hide at the beginning. I know I did. A lot has changed for me since the day I tentatively clicked on *Send* and my first post whizzed away and hit the forum.

Stop Trying to be Normal

What is this *normal* thing we're so focussed on? I think we have to let it go. We have to do our own thing despite the raised eyebrows. Gradually, you will change as you get used to interacting and eyebrows won't fly up so often. You can only achieve a change if you let go of that dog on a leash that's trying to pull you to a normal that doesn't exist.

No one is really normal. And that's just as well, because normal is boring.

Act the Beliefs You Want

You might want to believe you will succeed, but you don't succeed – not at first. Never mind. You can start by pretending.

Act the self-confidence you'd like to have. In the end, it will become real. You will gradually start to believe in your ability to succeed. Even before that happens, other people will believe it. Faking self-confidence at a job interview might well get you that job.

Love Yourself

Because only by loving yourself can you believe that you're worthy of reaching out and receiving help. Only by loving yourself can you believe you're worthy of being heard in a conversation.

And you *are* worthy. We all are. The world is missing something by not noticing you, by not hearing your contribution to society.

Believe that you deserve friendship, respect and happiness.

Try, Try and Try Again

You won't succeed on the first attempt. If you're not used to talking, it won't come out right the first time you try this new thing. Try again. And again. Eventually, it'll start to get better.

Who said life was easy?

Appendix

Books and Links

I've said all I have to say. I'm going to leave the last word to the experts, by listing a few books and links recommended by SAers. These are all in English and the comments were written by different SAers, including me.

Books

A few of the many books available. Most are specifically orientated towards SA, while others address related issues, such as panic attacks, depression and anxiety.

Overcoming Social Anxiety and Shyness, 2nd Edition: A self-help guide using Cognitive Behavioural Techniques
By Gillian Butler, published by Robinson (2016)

The first half of the book explains SA, what it's like, how it's self-perpetuating, and what causes it. The second half looks at methods of dealing with it: changing thinking patterns, doing things differently, reducing self-consciousness, building up confidence etc. It's pretty good, but you really have to motivate yourself to follow the exercises. This is the book most often recommended by UK SAers.

Diagonally-Parked in a Parallel Universe: Working Through Social Anxiety
By Signe A Dayhoff, published in USA by Effectiveness-Plus Publications (2013)

From the book cover:
"Alleviate your social anxiety pain. Improve your daily functioning. Work toward your potential. ... You will discover

how to significantly and effectively: Reduce your fear of evaluation, negative thinking, anger, and embarrassment. Raise your self-confidence and social effectiveness at work and play. Say good-bye to your loneliness, make friends, and date more comfortably. Control your stress and deal with criticism, disagreements, and rejection. Make the impression on others you want them to have. Create your own career opportunities."

The author herself says she suffered from SA, yet has successfully worked through it. She describes SA and various related disorders; possible origins and triggers of SA; discusses CBT, psychologists and medications; and offers advice on dating and jobs.

"This self-help book didn't change my life (as numerous gushing reviews on amazon.com led me to believe before I purchased the book), but it did give me more insight on SA."

Feeling Good: The New Mood Therapy
By David D Burns, published by Harper (2012)

"The book is actually aimed at people suffering from depression, and uses CBT. There is a good section on identifying different kinds of thinking disorders. Not all of the book is necessarily relevant to an SAer. There is stuff about raising your self-esteem, dealing with 'Do Nothingism', taking criticism, handling anger, defeating guilt, how to distinguish between depression and sadness, and, especially useful for SA, 'The Approval Addiction', and more besides. Again it's pretty helpful, and gives a little more detail on cognitive distortions and further ideas on how to combat them than the Butler book, but you need to be motivated."

Cognitive Therapy of Anxiety Disorders: A Practice Manual and Conceptual Guide
By Adrian Wells, published by Wiley (2013)

Adrian Wells provides here a comprehensive overview of the cognitive model of anxiety disorders and illustrates how detailed, disorder-specific cognitive conceptualisations inform the choice of therapeutic interventions. It is intended for therapists, but SAers have also found it very useful.

Feel The Fear And Do It Anyway
By Susan Jeffers, published by various publishers including Ebury Digital (2017)

A book of advice on how to cope with fear of various kinds of experience, such as public speaking, self-assertion, decision-making, intimacy, being alone, ageing, losing a loved one, and ending a relationship. Some of it can sound foreign to British ears.

Overcoming Low Self-Esteem
By Melanie Fennell, a series published by Robinson (2006-2009)

Contains CBT techniques which can help with SA, although it doesn't specifically refer to SA.

Depression – The way out of your prison
By Dorothy Rowe, published by Routledge (2003)

A UK book recommended by those who don't usually like self-help books. Rowe's books have apparently changed a lot of people's lives.

Awaken the Giant Within: How to Take Immediate Control of your Mental, Emotional Physical and Financial Life
By Anthony Robbins, published by Simon & Schuster (2012)
Recommended to help you take control of your emotions, be driven by your desires, focus on what you want and the find the solution to that.

Been There, Done That? DO THIS!
By Sam Obitz, published by Super Tao Inc. (2003)

"Short and simple like a For Dummies book but written from a sufferer's POV. The TEA forms* in it have helped me immensely and continue to help me."

(* A TEA form is a type of automatic thought page, similar to the one shown in Chapter 6.)

Overcoming Your Child's Fears and Worries
By Cathy Creswell and Lucy Willetts, published by Robinson (2007)

Recommended by Sofi Marom (see Chapter 2).

Fiction

I've read one work of fiction in which a main character had social anxiety: *The Mill River Recluse* by Darcie Chan. It's a lovely, well-told story. It certainly kept me turning the pages. The story is believable, has believable characters and deserves to be read. However, I have some reservations about it.

Mary, the recluse, has social anxiety. The reason for this is mentioned three times in the book (which I thought a bit excessive) and relates to one terrible incident that occurred when she was sixteen. She mentions that she was always shy, but I still think this is too easy. One incident, however bad, doesn't cause social anxiety on its own. There has to be a lot more than that. I would have liked to have heard much more about Mary's childhood and what led to her condition.

The consequence of Mary's anxiety – becoming a recluse seen generally by only one other person and later by two others – is a very extreme outcome of social anxiety. This is mentioned in the book by a professional who meets her and says, "I've never seen such an extreme case of social anxiety."

Most people with social anxiety don't keep themselves completely hidden in that way. They force themselves to get out and function in society, however much of a struggle that is. I think someone who reads of an extreme case like this could make light of the effort made by someone who appears to function fairly normally.

Links

Internet sites come and go, and the best way of knowing which are current is to search for 'social anxiety' or 'social phobia'. Most sites contain links to many other sites.

Address	Title	Content
www.social-anxiety.org.uk/	Social Anxiety UK	Information Personal stories Chatrooms Online Forum Comprehensive list of links The forum is moderated and hence keeps out offensive posts.
www.socialanxietysupport.com/	Social Anxiety Support	Information Online Forum
www.anxietyuk.org.uk/	Anxiety UK	Includes information on social anxiety
www.socialphobiaworld.com	Social Phobia World	Information Personal stories Online Forums The forums are not moderated.

www.socialanxietyinstitute.org/	Social Anxiety Institute	US site specialising in the treatment of social anxiety, including:
		    Information
		    Personal stories
		    Chatroom
		    Videos
		    Audio therapy

www.socialanxietyassist.com.au/	Shyness & Social Anxiety Treatment Australia	A variety of information, including therapists, courses and support in Australia.
socialanxietyireland.com/	Social Anxiety Ireland	All aspects of social anxiety in Ireland.
www.ntw.nhs.uk/pic/selfhelp/	Northumberland, Tyne and Wear NHS Self-Help Guides	Helpful, comprehensive information on various topics, including social anxiety and depression.
stigmafighters.com/stigma-fighters-miriam-drori/	Pressing the Button on Stigma Fighters	My experience with the stigma of having SA.

Fantastic Books
Great Authors

CROOKED
CAT

Meet our authors and discover
our exciting range:

- Gripping Thrillers
- Cosy Mysteries
- Romantic Chick-Lit
- Fascinating Historicals
- Exciting Fantasy
- Young Adult and Children's
  Adventures
- Non-Fiction

Visit us at:
www.crookedcatbooks.com

Join us on facebook:
www.facebook.com/crookedcatbooks

Made in the USA
Columbia, SC
16 September 2017